This book was created for congregations to pore over and use as a reference that is both accessible and interesting. It was imagined primarily with small and mid-sized congregations (with and without clergy) in mind. Hopefully, larger congregations will find it interesting and helpful, too.

In the early 1970s, I was invited by the Ford Foundation to participate in a national brain trust focusing on program development for girls and women in math and science. Unsure of what to expect, I arrived at Asilomar Conference Center in Monterey, California.

Gathered there was a rich collection of men and women, professionals in program development. This brain trust spent a week in beauty and comfort, all amenities provided, all needs met. As each day unfolded, we had only to talk, share experiences, inspire one another, and be creative. Facilitators recorded our ideas, and took them away to make use of them. The idea of engaging a panel of experts, a Pacific Northwest District brain trust, to create the basic structure of *Churchworks* stemmed from this experience.

Two decades later, I attended a seminar: "The Learning Game," presented by Educational Discoveries, Inc. It explored program and training design through the use of metaphor. The seminar based its learning model on the work of Dr. Paul MacLean, chief of the Laboratory for Brain Evolution and Behavior at the National Institute for Mental Health in Bethesda, Maryland, in 1952. Dr. MacLean developed a *triune brain model* that described three major functional brain systems: reptilian, limbic, and cortex.

The most primitive area is the *reptilian*, governing instinctive behaviors such as sex, territory, and aggression. The *limbic* governs basic emotions such as fear, joy, sadness, love, and hate. The *neo-cortex* governs and processes functions such as sight, hearing, speech, math, music, and thinking. The cortex also integrates emotions with thoughts.

The model the seminar offered was seated in the notion that the more of the brain involved in a learning experience, the deeper, more lively, and more successful the learning experience will be. Metaphor is one way to involve more of our brain in a learning experience. *Churchworks*, a book about congregational health, merges insights from these learning events.

All gratitude to the support of the Unitarian Universalist Funding Panel, the encouragement of the Pacific Northwest District Board, the imagination of the Pacific Northwest District Chapter of the Unitarian Universalist Minister's Association, the embracing hospitality of the Seabeck Conference Center, and Dr. Connie Celum, physician and friend, who read the manuscript for physiological correctness and then said *Churchworks* was for *more than churches*.

The creativity, experience, energy, and spirit of the *Churchworks* brain trust began the process that produced this book. Without the brain trust, this book wouldn't have happened. The members of the Pacific Northwest District brain trust include: Jackie Buckley from Alaska; Bill Jones, the Reverend Sydney Morris, and Doug Sabourin from British Columbia; the Reverend Jill McAllister and Judi McGavin from Oregon; Cathy Cartwright, Peter Henrickson, the Reverend Lucy Hitchcock, the Reverend William Houff, the Reverend Jaco ten Hove, and Porter Kelley from Washington.

Art and group graphics were contributed by Sinclair Crockett, a creative and talented co-conspirator from long ago.

Introduction

Since the early days of Christianity, the church has been referred to as the "body of Christ." Unitarian Universalist congregations sing, "standing here in one strong body." What does it mean for a congregation to be a strong body? At a chapter meeting of the Pacific Northwest District Unitarian Universalist Minister's Association, we explored this metaphor. The collegial group brainstormed possible tables of contents for this book using the body metaphor.

Self-help books (such as *How to Repair Your Own VW* and *Our Bodies, Our Selves*) informed the developmental process. I wanted *Churchworks* to be both interesting and accessible—like these pioneering books. Hopefully, *Churchworks* will be useful as a way to take charge of the health and well-being of your congregation.

Imagine a congregational body as a gathering of religious people, living as part of a religious community. But remember that the model is ultimately a metaphor, one intended as a teaching tool rather than a description of the literal or even virtual church.

WHAT IS A WELL CONGREGATION?

Imagine the finest human body you can—perhaps a world-class athlete, someone at your local gym, a friend. What makes those bodies strong, healthy, and beautiful? The answer is likely a combination of exercise, relaxation, nutritious food, challenging and useful work, engagement in life, the love and support of family, colleagues, and friends, and plenty of stimulation. And a life of the spirit!

Isn't it likely that a "well" congregation knows how to join in the satisfactions of shared work; to relax, worship, and meditate together; to be stimulated, supported, and challenged to personal growth; to exercise its social, learning, and justice muscles; to receive intellectual, spiritual, and emotional stimulation; to be well fed by the time, talent, and treasure of its members? However, each congregational body, like each individual, has worth and dignity. To be human is to be imperfect—the idea for this book is health, not perfection.

HOW TO USE *CHURCHWORKS*

Churchworks is connected to the Unitarian Universalist Association, whose mission is to serve its member congregations. We hope this book will help you develop a familiarity with and a passion for our larger community.

Every culture and people have their own perspectives and customs. The exploration of our lives and learning about the lives of others opens us to the possibilities of a larger beloved community. We want *Churchworks* to encourage an expanding sensitivity to these possibilities.

The liberal use of lists of possibilities is a way to expand your resources. Browse. Start anywhere. Take what you can use and use it. And let us know if you have ideas to add. Recommended readings at the end of each chapter suggest deeper explorations.

The Roshi said, "What is sickness? What is health?"

Brain

CHAPTER ONE

Core Documents for Your Congregation

The brain, safe inside the skull, is where the body organizes and stores its information. Every congregation should have a basic core of information about itself, organized and stored in a safe place. In the human body, such information is encoded into the smallest units of the body. In a congregation, such vital information must be affirmed by and available to every member of the congregation. It is information that a congregation would need if the building were flooded or burned down, or if important documents were lost or stolen. This chapter will help you identify the core information that your congregation should have and keep safe. The metaphor of the brain suggests ways in which these core documents might be discerned and organized.

Always store these documents in a safe place—one copy of each should be kept inside your building and a second copy outside, in a safe deposit box.

BYLAWS

First among valuable documents are the bylaws, which are the official beginnings of congregations. Bylaws describe the details by which congregations are structured. Bylaws are about governance, as distinguished from policy. Policies deal with finance, personnel, building use, and so on. Each congregation (in accordance with different countries, states, and provinces) constructs its own bylaws. Your congregation began when it formed a Bylaws Committee. Its members became knowledgeable about local requirements and constructed congregational bylaws. Your congregation voted its approval. The Bylaws Committee met after that for periodic review and preparation for submission of bylaw revisions to the congregation. If you are a brand-new congregation, forming a Bylaws Committee should be one of your first tasks. There are major categories of bylaws to consider, and questions to ask and answer in bylaws.

COVENANT AND/OR PURPOSE

- What is the purpose and/or covenant of the congregation?
- What references do your bylaws make to the Unitarian Universalist Association and your District? (Specify your congregation's relationship to the larger Unitarian Universalist community.)

MEMBERSHIP

- Some congregations admit members with only one requirement: sign the book. However, a congregation with property could be taken over by a group of people coming in and just signing the book. Most congregations know that being a member costs a congregation money—operating expenses, Unitarian Universalist Association and District dues, staff costs, religious education costs, music, etc. It is important that potential members understand this and that the bylaws define the responsibilities of membership and stewardship.
- What are the conditions of membership in your congregation?
- Is a member anyone who comes in the door and signs the book?
- Is a member a person who pledges and/or makes a contribution of record? If so, what minimum amount, if any, is required?
- Is a member a person who agrees with the Unitarian Universalist Association Principles and Purposes or a covenantal congregational code of conduct?
- Must a person attend new member classes in order to join?
- How is a person admitted into membership? By an official vote of the board? (State the percentage required for approval of membership.)
- How is a person removed from membership (when a person dies, moves away, when they notify the church in writing of their resigna-

tion, when they do not make a pledge or a contribution of record, when they participate in behaviors unacceptable to the congregation such as child abuse, sexual misconduct, etc.)? By what percentage vote of the board, or membership (if any), is a person removed from membership? Usually the board votes members into and out of membership. There are legal problems if your bylaws do not specify how to remove people from membership.

CONGREGATIONAL MEETINGS

- How many congregational meetings a year will your congregation hold?
- How will your congregation define a quorum?
- What are your criteria for calling a congregational meeting?
- How must the members be notified of a congregational meeting and in what time period before the meeting?
- How are special meetings called?
- What advance notice do members need for a special congregational meeting to be called?
- Do the notice and agenda need to be in writing?
- Will they be mailed to members, published, or both?

AMENDMENTS TO THE BYLAWS

- How are amendments made to the bylaws?
- What percentage of votes of the quorum, and / or of the membership, is required to pass a bylaw?
- What are the procedures and timeline for bringing bylaw revisions to congregational meetings?

THE BOARD AND ITS OFFICERS

- What is the length of the term of the board?
- What are the conditions for the election of its officers? (If board members are expected to be liaisons to committees, say so. If they are

expected to sit on standing committees, say so. If your board will have *ex officio* members, state who they are—such as the minister or the treasurer and why.)

- What is the selection or nominating process for board nominees? What are the job descriptions of the president or moderator, vice president, secretary, and treasurer (in many congregations, the treasurer is appointed and *ex officio*, rather than elected), trustees-at-large (if any)?
- Is a board member required to be a member of the congregation?
- How many board members will there be? The use of wording such as "no fewer than, and no more than" allows for growth.
- How will terms of board members be staggered?

STANDING COMMITTEES OF THE BOARD

God is in the details.

- What are the standing committees of the board? Finance, personnel, long-range planning, building and grounds, and canvass are typical board committees in larger congregations. If you are just starting out, you may wish to include them in your bylaws. Provide a brief description of each committee you include.
- Will the board, as is generally the case, appoint committee chairs? If not, how will committee chairs be appointed?
- What are the terms of committee chairs?
- How many consecutive terms may they serve?
- How can they be removed from their appointment?

THE MINISTERIAL SEARCH COMMITTEE

- How is the Ministerial Search Committee elected?
- How many members will it have?
- What are its tenure and purpose?

THE COMMITTEE ON MINISTRY

- The Committee on Ministry (COM) is not a committee of the board, but a committee of the congregation in special relationship to the board.

- What are the conditions for the appointments of COM's members? What are their terms of office?
- What is the specific nature of their responsibilities? (Such as support and advocacy for the minister and the ministry of the congregation, evaluation facilitation, communication among the minister, staff, board, and congregation. You may wish to consult Chapter 8, "Heart: Creating and Nurturing Ministry," for extensive descriptions of different committee types.)

THE NOMINATING COMMITTEE

Almost always, the Nominating Committee is a committee of the congregation and is elected by it. It is important that it represent the diversity of the congregation. Describe the intent to select nominees for the Nominating Committee. State that full consideration will be given to the importance of diversity, previous service to the congregation, knowledge of the denomination and district, knowledge of church constituencies and congregation organization, willingness to be trained, respectfulness, and knowledge of who is interested in which areas of church life.

- How and when will the Nominating Committee be elected?
- What are the terms of committee members?
- Do members have staggered terms? Describe.

MINISTRY

- What are the powers, duties, and responsibilities of the minister?
- Have you guaranteed freedom of the pulpit?
- What are the conditions for calling a minister?
- What percentage of votes at a congregational meeting is necessary to affirm that call? Refer to the *UUA Settlement Handbook* for more information.
- How much and what kind of lay participation will exist in the congregation's shared leadership?
- How is this participation identified and covenanted?

- How will the congregation evaluate the minister?
- What are the procedures and terms for ending a called ministry?

CONGREGATIONAL POLICIES BOOKS

Every board sets policies on areas such as equal employment opportunity, the general use of the building, and finances. If your congregation does not have a policies book, appoint a task force with a member of the board to review board minutes for the last five to eight years. Ask them to:

- Pull out policies passed by the board.
- Mark those policies that have been superseded, by writing "superseded" in the margin, and the date of the action. Do not include superseded policies in the current policy manual. Remove obsolete policies.
- Organize the current, active policies by topic and section. Write one policy per page so that they can be easily inserted or removed without disrupting the book's structure. These comprise your congregation's policy manual.
- Include a copy of this manual in every board notebook.
- Update the policy book annually.

Ask your District Office for help if you need it: They can refer you to a congregation with a working policy manual.

PROCEDURES BOOK

Congregational procedures establish how policies and congregational business are carried out; they describe how certain tasks, which require definition, are to be accomplished. Procedures books are organized by topic: office procedures, purchasing procedures, building rental procedures, financial procedures, etc.

If you do not have a procedures book, appoint a task force to collect the procedures in your congregation and to write one. Choose people who have experience with this kind of work. You can ask your District Office for help or referral to a congregation that has a good procedures book as a model.

PERSONNEL MANUAL

A personnel manual details the policies and procedures for hiring, firing, supervising, evaluating, and maintaining staff. It includes sections on benefits, sick time, vacation time, grievance procedures, supervision, evaluation, and so on. A personnel manual states who is eligible for employment—members or not?—and describes the process for hiring and firing and developing contracts and letters of agreement. It also helps you to conform with national, provincial, and state equity laws and fair employment practices. Organizing this manual with one topic per page makes it easier to read.

If your congregation has employees and no personnel manual, ask the board to appoint a task force (preferably with members of the congregation who have experience in personnel matters) to draft one for the board to review and adopt. Call your District Office for help.

BOARD MANUAL

All board members need to receive a board manual to help them do their job. Board manuals are most frequently organized in a large (three-inch) three-ring binder with cover pockets. Dividers tell the board members where to look for reference and information: finance and budgets, calendar, minutes, bylaws, policies, congregational directory, and forms such as work requests and expense reimbursements. The board may appoint a task force to create a manual if it does not have one. Ask for help from the congregation—some folks love doing this kind of task. Three-hole punch all materials that are distributed to board members. You may wish to color-code sections for easier reference.

Ask your District Office if they can refer you to a nearby congregation with a good board manual to look at. Some districts provide a model board manual for congregations to consult.

VOLUNTEER GUIDELINES

Volunteer guidelines include job descriptions (one per page) for lay positions, such as committee chairs, the newsletter editor, office volunteers, and so on. These descriptions spell out specific expectations, including time commitments and the term of office for each position and how often the appointment is renewable. Guidelines also include committee descriptions (one per page), how members of each committee will be selected and appointed, the terms of office for committee members, and how often the terms are repeatable. Also included are descriptions of the board's or staff's responsibility for evaluating chairpersons and committee members, accountability and review procedures, and the role of staff members in relation to volunteers.

MAINTENANCE MANUAL

The maintenance manual is the "brain bank" of the building and the grounds. It should include:

- Copies of the deed, bills of sale, and any documents related to the building.
- Schematics for all building systems, such as water, heat, gas, electricity, showing where on-off switches and shutoff valves are located.
- Copies of insurance policies as well as warranties and instruction books for all equipment in the building, including stoves, heaters, mixers, dishwashers, vacuum cleaners, tools, office equipment, computers, and so on. A list of phone numbers for repair or resource persons for all of the above.
- Long-range financial plans for the ongoing development of major maintenance reserves and a major maintenance plan.
- Specifications for who has access to the building, how access to keys is determined, and how often building locks need to be re-keyed.
- Building use policies: Who will use the building, at what rates, and for what periods of time? Who arranges and approves rental and use permits?
- Policies on member and non-member usage, and whether different rates apply for profit, non-profit, and private users.
- Policies for member and non-member weddings, memorial services, and other rites of passage.
- Policies about smoking, alcohol, and drugs.
- Lists of all rental and use costs, including cleaning and damage

deposits as well as policies on major abuse of the building.

Reproduce at least ten copies of your maintenance manual. Store one copy in a safe place, *outside* the building, for emergency reference. Keep one copy inside the building, on file, and a second copy on the office bookshelf. One copy should be distributed to each member of the Building and Grounds Committee; one copy should be given to the custodian or sexton. If you do not have a maintenance manual, call your District Office for a model.

FINANCIAL POLICIES, PROCEDURES, AND GUIDELINES

Every Finance Committee needs to ask the important questions, define the answers, and put them into guidelines for members and staff.

TWENTY QUESTIONS TO ASK ABOUT CONGREGATIONAL FINANCIAL POLICIES

1. What will the fiscal/financial calendar year for the congregation be?
2. Where will the money to support the basic operating costs of the congregation come from? What percentages should come from pledges, collection, special fundraisers?
3. How will fundraising be done and scheduled? By whom? How will goals be set?
4. Could endowment money ever be used to support the basic operating costs of the congregation? If so, under what circumstances?
5. How is the board responsible for the endowment or building fund? What guidelines exist?
6. How is the board responsible for investments? What guidelines exist?
7. Who can sign checks? Should we have double signatures?
8. Who develops the budget and how? Who is consulted and in what order? What are the timeline and budget development process? Who approves the budget—the board, the congregation, or both?
9. How often will we have outside, scheduled financial audits? How often will we schedule informal, internal audits?

10. What kind of unified statement or report is required to show all of the congregation's finances and assets? How often is the report made? Who receives the report?

11. Can committees have separate bank accounts from the congregational account? Can committees raise money and under what circumstances? Is the money the property of the committee or the congregation? How long does that money stay with the committee—one budget year or more?

12. Do committees have the authority to spend money beyond their budget? If so, by what amount? Does the board? The staff? The minister? What are the limits of non-approved spending?

13. Can money be shifted from one area to another? By whom—minister, board, committee? Who determines where the money gets charged?

14. How will special funds, designated funds, gifts, and planned gifts be defined and handled? What are the conditions for accepting special funds or gifts? How is it determined whether conditional gifts will be accepted?

15. Are members fully or partially reimbursed for church-related travel and expenses? What procedures will they need to follow for reimbursement? Are receipts and mileage records required for reimbursement? By when will they be paid? Is there any limitation on when they may submit requests for reimbursement?

16. Will members, if they are delegates, be reimbursed for travel and expenses for district annual meetings or for General Assembly? Will training expenses for volunteers be reimbursed? Is training a budget line item for staff and laity?

17. Does the minister have a discretionary fund? How much and for what purpose? Has the difference between the minister's salary, housing allowance, benefits, and the "cost of the office" (such as expenses, travel, continuing education, etc.) been clearly delineated?

18. Will members and non-members be charged different fees for events?

19. Will we charge fees for religious education? For children of mem-

bers? For children of non-members? For lifespan religious education services such as adult classes? How would that money be used?

20. Will we charge non-members subscription fees to the newsletter? If not, how long will they receive this "gift subscription"? Will "friends" (non-members who attend regularly and may even pledge but don't join) be charged subscription fees? What about pledging friends?

LONG-RANGE PLANNING AND COVENANTS

Many congregations have specific processes developed for long-range planning. They create a notebook, which every member of the (ongoing) long-range or strategic planning committee has. The notebook can include timelines, definitions of goals, objectives, action steps, models of congregational surveys, and minutes from past long-range planning committee meetings. The notebook also includes copies of past long-range plans, with the congregation's accomplishments checked off and goals not accomplished flagged for future reconsideration.

Your District Office can help you develop a long-range planning committee and process if you do not have them already, or put you in touch with a nearby congregation that has a working committee and good process.

Conflict management and prevention procedures and a congregational code of good relations are described in Chapter 9, "Liver: Dealing with Congregational Conflict." If you have them, you should keep a copy of each of these in your brain bank, too. If not, you should create them.

MORE GOOD STUFF TO READ

The Commission on Appraisal of the Unitarian Universalist Association. *Interdependence: Renewing Congregational Polity.* Boston: Unitarian Universalist Association, 1997. The commission's report on congregational polity, including recommendations on governance and the relationship between congregations and the Association, asks that we "clarify and renew our understanding of congregational polity."

Merkert, Angela J. *A Process Tool to the Congregational Handbook*. The *Handbook* has no index, so this valuable addendum is a great help in identifying topics and pages.

Peers, Lawrence X., ed. *The Congregational Handbook: How to Develop and Sustain Your Unitarian Universalist Congregation*. Boston: Unitarian Universalist Association, 1995. Meant as a reference and guide, outlines the responsibilities of being a member congregation of the UUA, provides a list of resources and services available to member congregations, and offers guidance on major dimensions of congregational life.

The Unitarian Universalist Association Committee on Ministerial and Church Staff Compensation. *To Sustain the Living Tradition: Final Report and Recommendations to Unitarian Universalist Congregations on Compensation and Benefits Practices*. Boston: Unitarian Universalist Association, 1995. Useful in developing congregational good employer policies.

Unitarian Universalist Association. *The UUA Settlement Handbook*. Please call the Department of Ministry at (617) 742-2100 to order. All about ministerial search and settlement.

Unitarian Universalist Minister's Association. *Guidelines for Unitarian Universalist Ministers, April 1998*. Includes the *Code of Professional Practice* and *Supplement for Ministers in Canada*. Contact the Unitarian Universalist Minister's Association, 25 Beacon Street, Boston, MA 02108, (617) 742-2100.

Breath and Spirit

CHAPTER TWO

Animating
Congregational Life

What is spirit? The origins and roots of the word *spirit* have to do with breath. Just as the body recycles air, taking in what it needs, letting out what is not useful, congregations can recycle sacred language. Words like *spirit, worship,* and *religion* are useful words.

Think about spirit. Think about breath. The presence of breath moves oxygen to every cell of the body. Without breath, the body cannot exist—it expires. Breath animates the body, gives life. In a congregational body, our spiritual life, as breath, animates us. To be lively, we must pay attention to the spiritual, the inspiring and aspiring moments and impulses of congregational life.

One of the great strengths of the Unitarian Universalist movement is pluralism. Embracing tolerance, congregations have welcomed and accepted people of many different perspectives. The Unitarian Universalist "spiritual body" ranges from one end of a theological-philosophical continuum to the other. See how diverse your congregation is by using the following spiritual continuum exercise.

SPIRITUAL CONTINUUM EXERCISE

Identify one end of the room as theist/Christian and the other end as atheist/ humanist. Ask people to imagine a line from one end to another. Tell them that that line is a continuum, and ask them to stand where they would place themselves on that continuum. (People who believe in some kind of god move toward the theist end. People who believe in some kind of life force move to the middle. Agnostics, atheists, and rational secular humanists stand at the other end, and so on.) Once everyone is in place, ask them to look around and to see how many different views exist within one congregation.

You could mention that congregations like King's Chapel in Boston and the First Unitarian Society of Minneapolis sit at far opposite ends of the continuum. They are two congregations rich with the history and noble with the traditions of Unitarian Universalism.

Next, ask people to imagine that one end of the room is identified as freedom, the other end as oppression. Ask them to place themselves on the continuum again. Do this activity several more times using some of the following values:

- compassion/self-interest
- acceptance/required creed/openness to all beliefs
- pro-choice/pro-life
- Democrats/other/Republican
- preservation of the environment/the environment is for our use.

You can make up your own values, too—a half dozen should be enough.

SHARED VALUES IN OUR RELIGION

The word "religion" has its roots in the Latin *religiare,* one meaning of which is *to bind.* Just as our pluralism inspires us and binds us in community, so are we a community of shared meaning, as exemplified by our shared values. An expression of these values is found in the Unitarian Universalist Association Principles and Purposes. It is useful to reacquaint ourselves with them periodically. They are printed at the back of this book.

Our challenge, however, when theological and philosophical differences divide us, is to understand that we are more alike than different and that what we share inspires and binds us. Try the following process with your congregation.

WHAT DO I BELIEVE? WHAT DO WE BELIEVE? EXERCISE

This absorbing and bonding exercise was developed by the Reverend Robert T. Latham to be used with an entire congregation to define their commonalities of belief. It provides participants with an opportunity to hear each other's stories and to open themselves to learning about different beliefs.

To begin, write the five Questions of Religion and Philosophy on newsprint in large letters, listing one question per sheet. Do not reveal the questions to the group until you are ready to read them aloud. Find a room with enough space and/or breakout space for groups of six to hold conversations where each person can be heard clearly. If you use the weekend, or the four-weeks-plus-Saturday format, you will need to order food. Ask a neighboring congregation to provide food and clean-up in exchange for the same services at one of their events. Do not ask participants to prepare food or to clean up. Provide free child care so that everyone can participate.

Welcome

Welcome everyone to the process, lighting a chalice and asking the participants to read the Principles and Purposes in unison.

Break the large group into groups of six. Do this by asking people to find one other person whom they do not know or do not know well. Then ask each pair to join up with two other pairs that they do not know well, making a group of six. Discourage couples and close friends from being in the same group.

Read aloud the following: "When someone asks you what you as a Unitarian Universalist believe, can you respond confidently and clearly? When you feel unhappy about where your beliefs are taking you, do you know what to change? A fundamental social principle is at work behind these questions. Only if we know our beliefs can we put them to work to create change in society or our own lives. The issue is control. We can only change what we know. There are many ways to approach our beliefs to define them. One way is to use the time-honored questions of religion and philosophy, which are fundamental to human existence. Their answers determine our values and shape our destiny. Every attitude and action of a person's existence reflects these questions. Everyone lives answers to these questions, whether they have defined them or not.

This exercise can be accomplished during a weekend retreat, over six 2 1/2-hour meetings, spaced one week apart, or in four 2 1/2-hour meetings and one full Saturday.

Newsprint

Magic markers

Masking tape

3" x 5" cards

Copies of the exercise for each person.

Copies of Principles and Purposes for each person (see Resource).

Chalice

"The purpose of religion is to speak and model a message that offers the power of wholeness in human relations and the inspiration of hope in human destiny. Where does this message come from? It is formed by a religion's answers to these questions. What distinguishes Unitarian Universalists and others is the answers we give to these questions.

"Look at the statement of Principles and Purposes by asking these questions and some of the beliefs we hold in common are revealed. Likewise these questions can expose what any fairy tale or children's story teaches. Ask these questions of any psychology or philosophy and its real message becomes apparent.

"These questions are a primal tool for understanding the meanings humans make, whether as individuals or as groups. The answers to these questions combine to form a view of reality, a filter through which experience is seen to create meaning."

Questions of Religion and Philosophy

1. Who am I? This is a question about human nature. Are we good or evil, worthy or unworthy, powerful or impotent, eternal or ephemeral, divided or whole?
2. How do I know what I know? This is a question about human authority. What is the ultimate source of our knowing? Does knowing derive from without or within humans? How do I know what I know? How do I know what I know is true?
3. Who or what is in charge? This is a question about our ultimate value. What is that which is greater than all else, that for which there is no beyond? What stands behind or within human existence? What is the dynamic operational principle, force, essence, or power that infuses creation with reality?
4. What is my purpose? This is a question about the source of my well-being and what sustains my sense of self-worth. Why do humans exist, and for what purpose? What gives life meaning and worth? How is one made whole or integrated? How are humans saved?
5. What does my death mean? This is a question about the boundaries of time in human existence. What happens to humans at death? What does death say about birth and living? What is the

nature of time? How does "in time" human existence affect death and beyond? Is there a redemption beyond death?

Defining and Sharing

Say to the group: "The purpose of this part of the exercise is not only to define our commonalities, but to increase our appreciation for the differences of belief among us."

Avoid debate and limit responsive dialog only to clarify the beliefs presented. Permit tolerance of these differences to affirm the freedom of belief that we cherish. Maintain a spirit of openness to differing expressions, which expand the reality of everyone present to encourage bonding rather than separation.

Distribute 3" x 5" cards to each person. Let each person in the group spend half an hour defining their individual answers to the first question and writing a response, using 30 or fewer words.

Exploring Commonalities

For each question, have the group go through this activity using a total of no more than two hours per question. After each person has defined and shared his or her answers, let the rest of the group list the commonalities they have discovered between the speakers' answers and their answers. These may be printed on newsprint, so that all can see them.

Let the group then identify the commonalities they have discovered between themselves and others in the group. Let the whole group discuss these commonalities. Note the strands of key concepts that are shared or largely shared by the whole group.

Ask the group to formulate and write a shared common response to each question. Say: "The key to success is to deal with concepts rather than favorite words. Avoid a simple listing of everyone's similarities. Try to develop words and/or phrases to act as an umbrella over the group's commonalities. Assume, as a group, that you are offering your final response to be published in a newspaper advertisement about what the group holds in common. Be clear and succinct, using no more than 30 words."

This is a consensus-seeking exercise. Again, avoid debate. To achieve consensus requires devotion to finding common ground and the willingness of the individual to bend for the sake of the whole.

At the end of each question, reconvene the whole group, and have each group share its final response.

Say to the group: "While there may remain some unresolvable differences, this exercise reveals that Unitarian Universalists generally hold far more in common than we do in difference. It is commonality, not differences, that bond us in community and give power to create social change."

TELLING OUR STORIES: A CONGREGATIONAL PROCESS

This one-time workshop works best with groups of no more than eight people. Participants will be sharing information about their life journeys and their journeys toward Unitarian Universalism.

Ingathering

Begin the session with the whole group together in a five-minute Ingathering. First light the chalice, singing "Come, Come, Whoever You Are" (hymn #188 in *Singing the Living Tradition*). Welcome the group, then distribute copies of the exercise.

Process

Read aloud the following instructions to the whole group before breaking into small groups: Each person should have about 15 minutes to speak. Let the timekeeper be the person to the left of the person speaking.

Ask each person to tell the story of how he or she came to this congregation by saying: "Were you born into a Unitarian Universalist congregation? If not, what was your religious history? How did you first hear about the Unitarian Universalist Association? What caused you to first come? What about this congregation was really moving to you? Tell us that story. Give an example or anecdote about the congregation that was meaningful to you. What inspired you to become a member of this congregation?"

Leave time for people to ask the speaker questions. Give each group a 15-minute warning when two hours are almost over. After the two hours are over, reconvene everyone in the large group. Ask for comments, observations, and feelings about what happened.

Three hours

Copies of the exercise for each participant

Copies of *Singing the Living Tradition*

Chalice

If more participants attend than expected, divide them into small groups at the beginning of the exercise.

Closing

Close the exercise by singing "From You I Receive" (hymn #402 in *Singing the Living Tradition*). Extinguish the chalice, saying: "Hold close to your heart the gifts of story we have received tonight. Love one another dearly, attend one another with deep respect, and let the gifts of compassion and understanding be with you, and with all of us, always."

SPIRITUAL SUPPORT GROUPS IN THE UU TRADITION

Two Unitarian Universalist ministers, Amanda L. Aikman and Mary Grigolia, believe there is a great hunger for safe spaces for spiritual exploration and support within Unitarian Universalist congregations. With that in mind, they designed a very simple process called Affirmation Circles that can be used by any group. The process works well as a community builder as well as for support groups. Aikman and Grigolia found that people with a great range of problems benefit from being in a group together.

This process encourages its users to improvise and create rituals and practices using the guidelines below as a base for finding the practices that best suit their group. The basic format, however, should be kept intact.

GUIDELINES FOR AFFIRMATION CIRCLES

- *Openness.* The groups are never closed in membership. Unlike other types of support groups, one need not have particular needs to belong.

  However, if someone proves to be disruptive or disrespectful of the guidelines, the group should state expectations and draw appropriate borders, including asking the person to leave. If someone is in crisis, the group may wish to refer the person to a minister or counselor for help.
- *Smallness.* The guidelines are designed for a group of four to seven people. If eight or more people show up, randomly divide them into groups of approximately equal size. This division should be done randomly, i.e., by having people count off: "1, 2, 1, 2" etc. around the circle. Then all the "'1's" might go into one room; the "2's" into another.

Copies of instructions for each person

Candle or chalice

Copies of *Singing the Living Tradition*

Flowers or cloth for the centerpiece

Choose the facilitator for the day. Distribute instructions to everyone.

- *Brevity.* The meetings should last no longer than an hour to an hour and a quarter. If the time limits specified in the guidelines are adhered to, everyone will have a chance to speak without using up the whole session. People may wish to stay longer and socialize after the formal part of the meeting, which should be optional.
- *Rotating leadership.* A different person should facilitate the group each time. All anyone needs to facilitate a meeting is a copy of these guidelines.

Chalice Lighting
Light the candle or chalice, inviting participants to read these words (or words of the facilitator's choosing) in unison:

May the light we now kindle
inspire us to use our powers
to heal and not to harm,
to help and not to hinder,
to bless and not to curse,
to serve you, Spirit of Freedom.

Opening Song
If you wish to sing a song, do it now before the reading. Here are suggestions from *Singing the Living Tradition*: #361, "Enter, Rejoice and Come In"; #396, "I Know This Rose Will Open"; #400, "Shalom, Havayreem"; #389, "Gathered Here."

Opening Unison Words
We come to this place, this time
With vulnerabilities, hurts, wounds, fears.
We come to this place, this time
With gifts, joy, love, laughter.

May we discern in one another's faces and voices
The spirit of all that is holy.
And may we, together, create a safe space
For healing and peace to enter our hearts.
So may it be.

"The unexamined life is not worth living."
—SOCRATES

Reading the Guidelines

Read aloud the guidelines to the group, or have the group share in the following reading. "This is an Affirmation Circle—a support group in the Unitarian Universalist tradition. All who are welcoming are welcome here; there are no criteria for attendance, except for a willingness to follow the basic guidelines and to respect the Unitarian Universalist Association Principles and Purposes—especially the first, 'the inherent worth and dignity of every person,' and the third, 'acceptance of one another and encouragement to spiritual growth in our congregations.' We ask that everyone respect the confidentiality of what is said here, and that everyone speak only from her or his experience. The only other ground rules are not to interrupt, not to give advice, and not to exceed the time limit for talking. Everyone is expected to share the responsibility for helping participants remember time limits. Everyone should feel free to share or not to share, as she or he wishes."

Ask for a volunteer to be timekeeper. The timekeeper's task is to keep track of the time limits designated in parentheses for specific activities, and to call out "time" softly, when the time limit has been reached.

Check In

Each participant has one minute to tell his or her name and what she or he brings to the group (an emotion, an event, a discovery, an insight, a memory, a thought).

Theme for the Day

See "Themes for Affirmation Circles" below for theme readings. More ideas can be found in the back of hymnals and on your bookshelves.

Have either the facilitator or a volunteer say the following: "Let's enter into a time of meditation and reflection, a time of silence, a time of deepening, as we reflect together for five minutes on today's theme." Then read the theme reading through slowly, twice.

Themes for Affirmation Circles

The purpose of the reading is to offer a theme for meditation. These short readings are from *Singing the Living Tradition*. You might want to read them aloud twice, quietly. Or offer your own readings. Participants might sit with a blank mind, focus deeply on the reading, or let their minds wander all over the place.

- "Surely the Lord is in this place—and I did not know it."—Genesis 28 (Where is the holy in your life today? Or if the word "holy" is not useful for you, where is the wholeness in your life?)
- "A gratitude had begun to sing in me."—Denise Levertov (Does gratitude sing in you? When? What is its song?)
- "Hold fast to dreams."—Langston Hughes (What are your dreams?)
- "Grant us the ability to find joy and strength."—Jewish prayer (Where do you find your joy and strength?)
- "Evoking the presence of the Great Compassion"—Thich Nhat Hanh

Silence   (5 minutes)

Talk about the Theme   (15 minutes)
Say to the group: "In the Quaker style, anyone who feels moved to do so may now speak about what he or she thought about during the silence."

Participants should feel free to respond to one another, but not to interrupt while others are speaking. Participants should not dominate the discussion. It is fine to just sit and listen, or for the whole group to remain silent during this time. After about half the time is up, encourage anyone who has not yet spoken to speak if he or she wishes.

Affirmation Time
Say: "Now we each have an opportunity to share with the group a need, prayer, wish, hope, or whatever is on our minds. It is often very healing to share concerns with a group, in a safe space. And it permits all of us to affirm one another, pray for one another, and hold one another in our hearts during the week. Let's go around the circle; each person will have three minutes to speak. Asking clarification questions is permitted but we will avoid giving advice. Mostly we will just listen to each person, and when each person has finished, join in our unison affirmation. Let us now take a minute of silence to see what our heart's desire is at this time in our lives, so that we can give full attention when others are speaking."

"No matter what our attempts to inform, it is our ability to inspire each other that enlivens and binds us. To inspire one another, we must know one another. The oxygen must get to every cell."

—PACIFIC NORTHWEST DISTRICT

BRAIN TRUST

Affirmation Requests and Responses

After each person has spoken for three minutes, the group affirms in unison and with vigor: "(Name), we hold you in our hearts, and we affirm your heart's desire. So may it be."

Closing Words and Song

Read the closing words in unison. You can stand and hold hands or put your arms around each other's shoulders at this time.

May the Love which overcomes all differences,
which heals all wounds,
which puts to flight all fears,
which reconciles all who are separated,
be in us and among us
now and always, Amen.
—Frederick E. Gillis

Here are suggestions for closing songs from *Singing the Living Tradition*: #396, "I Know This Rose Will Open"; #402, "From You I Receive"; #409, "Sleep My Child"; #413, "Go Now in Peace"; #474, "As We Leave This Friendly Place."

Extinguishing the Chalice

You can blow out the chalice by yourself or include the entire group.

WORSHIP AND HOW IT IS ORGANIZED

The word, "worship" has its origins in the notion of worth. Gathering on Sunday mornings or at any other time is about that which has worth, is worthy. Worship stands at the center of congregational life; doing it with grace and effectiveness provides great possibilities for inspiration and the life of the spirit. Sunday mornings bring a religious community together in body and spirit. Although this book is not intended as a worship manual, information about and preparation for services can make our life of the spirit (and services) smoother and our experiences richer and more meaningful.

This section is divided into three parts:

- basic elements of an order of service
- preparation for congregations who are preparing to welcome a guest into their pulpit
- 20 do's and don'ts for services.

Good services, on Sunday or at any time, have balance and symmetry, clear beginning, middle, and end. Their elements are inspired by music, readings, the lighting and extinguishing of a chalice or candle, and so on.

THE BEGINNING OF SERVICES

Words of Welcome

It is good to have a formal opening, letting people know that the service is starting. The welcome period is a good time to introduce and also welcome special guests, the pulpit speaker, or special musicians. Opening words usually come from the minister, the person who presides, or the lay worship leader. In some congregations, board members rotate this responsibility. Some congregations have ritual words of welcome that are said each time. The person opening the service should give his or her name and say the name of the congregation in the first few sentences. Sample opening words of welcome are:

> Good morning! (Leave time for people to respond, "Good morning!") My name is _____ and I want to welcome you to the Unitarian Universalist Congregation of the Mountains. We hope that you will join us after the service for coffee and conversation, and that you will find words here that move the mind and heart, a place of solace, comfort and community, and encouragement to pursue your spiritual journey.

> Good morning and welcome to the First Universalist Church of Eastown. I am _____, a member of the board of this congregation. All who come are welcome here. We hope that you will feel free to ask questions and to come again and again. Please join us for a social time after the service in the Fireside Room.

Good morning. My name is _____. The Unitarian Society of the Plains welcomes you. If you are old or young, male or female, we welcome you. If you are part of a family or a single person, we welcome you. If you are gay or straight, we welcome you. Whatever your color, ethnicity, or class, we welcome you. We hope you will find us an accepting and supportive faith community. We hope you will return, and should you choose to become a member, we will welcome you formally among us.

Announcements

Try having no—or very few—announcements and just savor the Sunday morning experience as a contemplative, uplifting, quiet time for body, mind, and spirit.

Announcements should be made at the beginning of the service and be as short as possible. Many congregations limit announcements to one or two urgent ones, and include others as part of the printed order of service. If your congregation must have announcements on Sunday morning, it is best to have one person (a lay leader) read them and to have a few clear guidelines, such as:

- Limit announcements to one paragraph, written out, one per group and one per person.
- No more than five announcements per morning, all of which should be timely and important to the whole community. Announcements of non-congregational activities can be placed on the bulletin board, in the order of service, or in a special section in the newsletter.
- Regular meeting announcements belong in the newsletter, not in a service.

Prelude

It is wonderful, restful, and healing to enter the sanctuary and to sit quietly listening to music. If you have musicians in your congregation, invite them to share their gifts. A prelude is usually soft music, setting a contemplative mood for the service. Peppy music with a beat, warm or uplifting music, or singing to learn the morning's hymns are also effective. Sometimes the minister or pulpit speaker will choose something appropriate to the morning's topic. Classical, new age, cool jazz, folk music, and others are fine, but the purpose of a prelude is centering.

Recorded music is fine, but be sure the person in charge of the sound system turns down the volume gradually before turning the system off. A loud pop at the end of a peaceful moment can be startling.

Call to Worship

The call to worship can be spoken by one person, by all in unison, or as an antiphonal reading (one person reads a line, then the congregation speaks the next line, and so on). Unison readings and antiphonal readings should be printed in the order of service.

Lighting the Chalice

Many congregations like to have a child light the chalice and rotate this responsibility among the children each week. Lighting a chalice or a special candle connects children to the larger Unitarian Universalist community. Different simple words can be spoken by a layperson or the minister each Sunday. Ritual words can be spoken by the minister, lay leader, or the whole community. It is bonding to use the same (unison) chalice-lighting response each week. Sample chalice-lighting words can be found in *Singing the Living Tradition*, or the person lighting the chalice may choose the words. A few sentences are usually enough.

Opening Hymn

Opening hymns gather people together, in song and spirit. They can also set the tone for the theme of the service. This is a good time for music that sings about community. There are many in *Singing the Living Tradition* such as #361, "Enter, Rejoice and Come In "; #360, "Here We Have Gathered"; or #358, "Rank by Rank."

Children's Time

This time is devoted to telling a story, having a conversation, or reading to children that relates to the topic of the sermon. The person who does this should be comfortable with children. The children may be invited to sit in the front of the sanctuary until it is time for them to leave. Most congregations sing the children out to a simple melody, like "Go Now in Peace." Some congregations like to join hands across the aisle, forming a bridge for the children to walk under as they exit to the religious education space.

Sharing of Joys and Concerns

Many congregations have a special time during the service when members speak about what is happening in their lives that is joyful, sad, or important. Often each speaker will light a candle while speaking. These moments are designed to be brief and personal: It is not a time for announcements. It is not a political time and should not be used to give an editorial. Some congregations, rather than lighting candles, move a flower or a rock from one container to another.

The lay leader or minister usually begins this moment by saying something like, "Now is the time in our community of shared faith to listen to the open hearts of our members, to share their joy and their sorrows, and to silently offer our own support and good wishes to them." He or she may light a candle for others to use to light their candles.

Some congregations have a special candelabra, or a bowl filled with sand to place the candles in. Usually seven, eight, or nine candles are enough. When all the candles are lit, the time for sharing is over. A final candle may be lit at the end, with the worship leader saying, "Let this last candle be lit for unspoken joys and concerns."

Some congregations, especially larger ones, have a table for candle lighting in the foyer where people can remember joys and concerns before the service begins. Often greeting cards or letters and envelopes are left there, so members can write greetings, letters of good will, or condolences. These are left there and mailed by the congregation's Caring Committee or family and friends.

THE MIDDLE OF SERVICES

Sharing of Responsibility

Collection can be taken early, in the middle, or at the end of the service. Some congregations put it at the beginning, just after the opening hymn, or before the children leave, and invite the congregants to use the time for greeting new people and old friends. Others do collection during special music, others following the sermon.

Whenever it is, collection should be intentional, with words about the opportunity to share in the responsibility for the good financial health of the community. Some congregations invite a member to speak these words, with a few sentences about the importance of the congregation in their lives.

Some congregations have the ushers hand the collection plate to the minister as a formal symbol of giving to the church; in other congregations, the ushers quietly leave when the collection is complete and bring the plate to the office to be counted. Some congregations, wanting new visitors to have no sense of obligation until they have been there a few times, say something like: "Those of you who are new are our guests this morning. We hope you will get better acquainted with us before you make the decision to share in this responsibility."

Hymn

Optional. If yours is a singing congregation, it will enjoy another opportunity to make music. This center hymn musically enriches the morning so it should bear some relationship to the morning's topic.

Readings

The readings on topics related to the morning's sermon are generally read by the minister (speaker) and / or the lay leader, and are brief (two to five minutes).

Meditation or Prayer

This is a time for silent contemplation, centering, being quiet inside oneself and with the community. Meditation usually lasts around three minutes, and can be started and ended by a bell.

Special Music

Performance of three to five minutes of music. Taped music is fine, but never as immediate as live music. The music usually should relate to the topic, or at least not contradict it.

Sermon

Usually lasts 12 to 20 minutes, depending on the speaker and the length of the service. The sermon is the centerpiece of the morning. Hopefully all that surrounds the sermon enhances it.

Closing Hymn

Usually has a direct relationship to the topic and gives voice to the congregation in response to the words that preceded it. An uplifting hymn is especially moving.

Closing Words or Benediction

"Benediction," in its Latin roots, means "good words." The closing words are an opportunity to speak these good words to or with the congregation. They are usually spoken by the minister, less often by the lay leader or the whole congregation, in unison. Some congregations like to join hands for the closing words. These words should be brief and meaningful.

Postlude

The postlude features closing music that is uplifting and formally closes the time of worship.

Congregational Response

Some congregations make a special time here for reflection and congregational response or sharing. Because many members prefer to experience the service quietly, response can be best after a service, rather than during it. Most congregations that have a talkback (the majority do not) invite those who are interested to get a cup of coffee and to meet in a special room. Usually the minister or pulpit guest joins them.

This is *not* a time to critique the minister or guest publicly but it is a time for members of the congregation to discuss the morning's topic.

PREPARING FOR A GUEST IN THE PULPIT

There are many gracious, considerate ways to welcome guests in your pulpit. Here are some suggestions.

- Appoint a Pulpit Guest Coordinator to facilitate the process from the time the guest receives an invitation from the Program or Worship

Committee until the final thank you. The Pulpit Guest Coordinator should serve on this committee.

- The committee inviting the guest gives the coordinator the name, address, and phone number of the guest as well as the date and topic of the sermon.
- The coordinator sends an initial letter of welcome to the guest, using the guest's ministerial title in the heading, but not in the salutation. A sample letter appears at the end of this list.
- Call the guest after you have received the order of service to say thank you and ask if he or she has questions. Let him or her know you look forward to hearing the speech. Call as a reminder if you do not receive the order of service promptly.
- Place the honorarium check in an envelope for the guest and make sure the guest receives it the morning of the service.
- Within a few days after the service, write a warm, brief thank-you note to the guest. Include any affirming feedback you may have heard.

Sample Letter of Welcome

Date
The Reverend Great Speaker (or The Reverend Dr. Great Speaker)
Address
City, State, Zip

Dear (Mr., Ms., or Dr.) Speaker,

The Unitarian Universalist Congregation of the Mountains is pleased to welcome you to its pulpit on October 21, 1998. I will be your contact person before and during your visit. Please call with any questions—if I don't know the answer, I'll find out.

Before your visit, and no later than September 10, we would appreciate your sending us a one-or-two paragraph biography and a two-or three-sentence description of your sermon topic to use in our newsletter.

I am enclosing several orders of service. Generally, we are flexible about how it is constructed. I have highlighted the elements that the congregation considers the core of our Sunday mornings. Please look them over, call me with questions, and send me your proposed order of service no later than October 11. Our services are rarely more than one hour long, with sermons between 15 and 20 minutes.

We welcome suggestions for music, and of course, the readings you want to include. If you would also like to do the opening and closing words, please let me know. We usually have a children's time early in our service. Please let me know if you would like to do this part or if a member of our congregation should do it.

Ms. Active Member will be your lay worship leader. She will meet you at the church at 10 A.M., one half-hour before the service starts, to familiarize you with our sanctuary. She will do the welcome, announcements, sharing of responsibility, and sharing of joys and concerns. Please let us know if you would like her to participate in the readings. We do not have a "talkback." Your honorarium will be $150; your transportation will be reimbursed at the rate of $.32 per mile. You will receive a check after the service.

We are eager to welcome you! We look forward to hearing you.

Sincerely,

Mr. First Welcomer
Pulpit Guest Coordinator
enclosures

TWENTY THINGS TO CONSIDER FOR SUNDAY SERVICES

1. About hymns: Try not to sing too many different hymns during one year. Choose one hymn always to be sung each Sunday of a month. Call it the Hymn of the Month. This way people will learn the music and build a repertoire of music.
2. Try having the musician play a medley of the hymns that will be sung in the service as a part of the prelude or preceding the prelude as people are entering. Train musical members of the congregation to teach and lead songs.

"Consider the inspiring, deep moments in a congregation's life; how one remembers them, how one pays attention to them, and aspires to more."
—PACIFIC NORTHWEST DISTRICT BRAIN TRUST

3. Be imaginative and adventurous. Art, theater, dance can all be a part of a Sunday morning. Use drums, flutes, tambourines, jazz—whatever works.

4. Test electronic equipment for sound levels, cues, and function right before the service.

5. Have two people proofread the orders of service *before* you print them. Check for spelling, correct names and titles, etc.

6. Encourage people not to applaud during the service as it can feel very disruptive. If they must applaud, ask them to hold their applause until after the postlude. However, different congregations have different styles and some may applaud at length.

7. Do a regular chalice lighting. Connect the lighting with the larger Unitarian Universalist community, saying things like: "Three hours ago in Portland, Maine, a chalice was lit. Two hours ago, in Rochester, Minnesota, a chalice was lit. One hour ago, in Santa Fe, New Mexico, a chalice was lit. And an hour from now, in Juneau, Alaska, a chalice will be lit. I light this chalice now, here, at this moment, connecting our congregation to all the member congregations of the Unitarian Universalist community."

8. Create a worship space that is lovely and thoughtful and reflects the personality of your congregation. Use flowers, cloths, and important pictures. Think about aesthetics, how it all fits together.

9. Try to have a time of silence and introspection: Most people need to be able to sit quietly and center. Try to educate people to be quiet once they enter the sanctuary. Make sure they have a good place to socialize afterwards.

10. Don't be afraid of emotion. Understand what the mood of the morning is about and consider how you can enhance it.

11. Some congregations do a one-minute "sound bite" on Unitarian Universalist history each Sunday to enrich their education about the roots and branches of our movement. This should be done at the beginning of the service.

12. Share the design of the service. Encourage your Worship or Sunday Service Committee to try things a few different ways—then get feedback from the congregation and use it.

13. Plan how the space will be organized. Experiment with new patterns like semicircles, using a traveling microphone, and so on.

14. Respect the differences and incongruities of beliefs and practices. Try to plan services so that all may comfortably participate and respond to what is happening most of the time.

15. Learn when and how to critique Sunday mornings. Sunday morning is not the best time. Rather, have the Worship or Sunday Service Committee regularly—but not too frequently—poll the congregation for its impressions.

16. Consider intention and practice in services. It is comforting and gives people a sense of ownership if they know they can depend on certain elements always to be a part of the service. Be sure to put clear directions, words, and explanations in the order of service so that newcomers will feel included.

17. To teach people how to meditate, focus one service on Buddhism and include simple instructions on meditation.

18. Although sharing Joys and Concerns is an important part of many congregations' worship, it can get out of hand. In one congregation, it went on so long there was no time for the sermon! So limit it, letting the worship leader say when the time comes, "This will be our last candle." Some congregations save Joys and Concerns until the end of the service.

19. Don't let your services run too long. One-hour maximum works best. Estimate time for each element in the service so you can know whether you need to cut. Let participants know clearly how much time they have.

20. Work backward: How do you want people to feel when they leave your service?

A CLOSING MEDITATION

Patrick T. O'Neill

So the newsprint is pulled down off the walls and gets folded up and fed into the computer that will turn all those random ideas into minutes, reports, letters, and brochures that prove we were here and what we saw and what we did.

And they get filed along with all the other newsprint sheets of all the other meetings that are the continuum of our lives. We could save all of them somewhere in the backs of memory until we're old and gray, you and I. And we could maybe leaf back through the pages someday, and read, and smile or cry at the work which claimed our energies and our creativity and our passions.

Someday, I suppose, we could gather them all up—the newsprint pages of our days—the stuff of our lives—and we could be tempted to think that somehow these various volumes of paper would be some kind of measurement: "Here. Here's what I did with those years. See, I put these words on these papers. And other people took these words and from them they made programs, and the programs changed their lives. It's all here, on the newsprint. Everything we did."

Well, not everything. Not everything. You can read the newsprint, but you can't read what it was like to be together in those years with that group of people. You can't read when we made each other laugh, or when we learned from each other in the process. That's not written on the newsprint, you see. All that stuff gets written elsewhere. It gets written on the heart. It shows up years later in a laugh line around the eyes. The newsprint doesn't record everything, you see.

The newsprint doesn't record the moments when we admired a colleague's skill, or when one paid us the honor of his or her attention, or told us we did a good job, or forgave us for small failures. Years from now the pages won't recall how the work bonded our friendships or made us better at home for what we did here, or what we received. That's material we have to stow away, each for him- or herself. Because if there's an ultimate summary to be had, it's not on the newsprint that records it. It's the heart and the face that will show how we spent our days.

The story is that the people in this group spent a portion of their years working on behalf of congregations. That's a good memory to stow away, something to feel good about—even if the newsprint doesn't tell the whole story or misspells our names. It's a fond and proud memory of you, dear friends, that I shall always treasure.

To me you will always be among the chosen candle lighters, taking the flame for a brief shining moment and passing it on to more and more and more.

"I enjoy the silence in a church before the service more than any sermon."

—RALPH WALDO EMERSON

A CLOSING RESPONSIVE READING

This reading, "The Artisan's Prayer," author unknown, was used at the Guthrie Theatre building dedication in Minneapolis, Minnesota. The group or congregation reads the capitalized lines and either the worship leader reads the lowercased lines, or each of the lowercase lines may be assigned to a different person to read.

TEACH ME
to use the time I have to work, and to use it well,
not losing a second.
TEACH ME
to profit from past errors
without succumbing to vain intransigence.
TEACH ME
to foresee my plans without torment,
to imagine my work without sorrow if it turns out
to be other than I had imagined.
HELP ME
when I begin my work; when I am at my weakest.
HELP ME
at the heart of my labor that I may hold tight the string of my attention.
AND MAY THIS COMMUNITY
HELP ME
FILL WITH HANDS AND HEARTS
THE GAPS IN MY WORK.
In all that I do, give me the strength and grace to speak to others and the
honesty to speak to myself.
GUARD IN ME
the integrity and hope without which I would lose heart.
PURIFY MY VISION.
WHEN I DO ILL, IT IS NOT CERTAIN THAT IT BE ILL.
WHEN I DO WELL, IT IS NOT CERTAIN THAT IT BE WELL.
Let me never forget
that all knowledge is in vain except where there is work.
And that all work is empty except where there is love.

And that all love is hollow which does not link me
to myself, to others, and to the universe.
TEACH ME
to give with my hands, my arms, my mind, my whole self.
REMIND ME
that the labor of my hands belongs to the future
and that all comes back to me through that which I have given.
REMIND ME
that if I work for the love of profit or power,
like a forgotten fruit I will rot in autumn.
REMIND ME
that if I work to please others,
like a flower in the grass I will fade in the evening.
BUT IF I WORK FOR THE LOVE OF GOOD,
THERE I WILL FIND MY PLACE,
FOR THE ONLY TIME TO DO GOOD IS HERE
AND NOW.

MORE GOOD STUFF TO READ

Buehrens, John A. and F. Forrester Church. *A Chosen Faith.* Boston: Beacon Press, 1998. An introduction to the Unitarian Universalist Association as a religious liberal organization that offers freedom of individual conviction and belief.

Unitarian Universalist Association. *Singing the Living Tradition.* Boston: Beacon Press, 1993. The newest Unitarian Universalist hymnal, a treasury of music and readings. If you do not already have a set of these hymnals, encourage your congregation to purchase them: People can buy one for their family, or in honor of a deceased family member or a member of the congregation. Bookplates to commemorate these gifts can be placed in the front of the book.

Skinner House Books, an imprint of the Unitarian Universalist Association, has a broad selection of meditation manuals that inspire Sunday morning services and deepen worship experience. For more information on Skinner House titles, call the UUA Bookstore at (617) 742-2100.

Circulatory System

CHAPTER THREE

Nourishing Healthy Congregations

Every minute, blood courses through our bodies, nourishing, protecting, transporting sustenance, regulating and protecting the systems that keep us alive and healthy. The circulatory system is a network in our body, delivering food and protection, carrying away poisons and waste, returning blood to the heart. Breath enlivens the blood with oxygen, and so rejuvenates it to do its work.

Think of members of the congregation as red blood cells. Imagine these members as they course through the building, engaged in the life of the congregation. When this circulatory system is flowing well, the body is healthy and communications flourish.

When the circulatory system is not flowing well, the body becomes unhealthy. Here are some signs that help identify a congregational circulatory system that is healthy or unhealthy.

Healthy	Unhealthy
Guidance for board; announcements are made at pulpit.	Worship service is verbose; clipboards float during service.
Every household is contacted regularly in some way.	No one visits shut-ins or hospitals; no member contact.
Library / bookstore has brochures and materials.	Nothing is available to inform and attract visitors about Unitarian Universalism.

Healthy (cont.)

Small groups are comfortable with "talking stick" process (passing a stick from person to person for 1-3 minutes).

Newsletter is crisp and follows guidelines.

Sparkling publications; logo is used creatively.

Joys and Concerns are personal, moving, and part of congregational life.

Adult religious education and affinity groups are full and prosper.

The building is used seven days and nights a week.

Unhealthy (cont.)

Full community does not communicate in congregational meetings.

Publications are sloppy and unrelated to each other.

Eyes commonly glaze over from a blur of print; no logo.

Announcements and editorials creep into Joys and Concerns.

Events are sparsely attended; there are no affinity groups.

The building is used mostly on Sunday mornings.

Healthy (cont.)	**Unhealthy (cont.)**
Canvass makes or exceeds goal.	Canvass never covers budget; asking for money is a drag.
Staff and committees feel supported and financially respected.	Congregation is unable to make routine purchases or pay staff timely. Expectations exceed capability, committees lack financial support.

CREATING HEALTHY MEMBERSHIP

Every congregation wants to have a membership that is involved and bursting with activity. To create healthy red blood cell members, the most important first step is to find out what people are eager to do.

"It's in the blood!"

- Some congregations circulate a form for members to fill in, such as an Enrichment Programs Survey.
- Some congregations have welcomers who interview new members and find out what interests them most.
- Some congregations have a graffiti board, where people can write up ideas and requests during coffee hour.
- Some congregations ask already existing groups to suggest possibilities for future membership activities.
- Some congregations collect newsletters and adult education flyers from other congregations and look through them for ideas.
- Some congregations have an Adult Programs Committee that may use the above techniques and then brainstorm the possibilities for the church year.

TWENTY SUGGESTIONS FOR ADULT PROGRAMS

1. Country and Western line dancing
2. Dreams and the meaning of dreaming

3. Parents' Group, meeting weekly for stay-at-home parents. Bring kids or not.
4. Weekend fishing trip for the men only (ages 13 to 100).
5. Women's ski trip
6. Wills and planned giving seminar
7. Healing service or affirmation circles
8. Artistic bookmaking: make journals, then start a journal group
9. Writer's workshop (poetry, prose, or fiction)
10. Monthly movies (the host chooses the movie), coffee and conversation or discussion following the film. Make popcorn.
11. Zen meditation at 8:30 Sunday mornings
12. River rafting for "chickens"
13. Uprooting racism for white people
14. Telling Our Stories groups
15. Owning Your Religious Past class
16. A roots study group, in which everyone talks about their ethnic origins
17. Make a Joyful Noise: singing for non-singers—learn hymns
18. An annual congregational camp. If you're a small congregation, invite a neighboring congregation to join you.
19. Earth-based spirituality seminar
20. Exploring Unitarian Universalism history class

In addition, every congregation has subcultures and special interest or affinity groups. Affinity groups become a bridge to intimacy as a congregation grows larger.

TWENTY AFFINITY GROUPS TO ORGANIZE

1. Spiritual direction
2. Singles
3. Couples
4. Cooking and eating group
5. Caregivers support group
6. Job search group

7. Internet chat group
8. Backpacking or paddling groups
9. Unitarian Universalist Humanists
10. Christian Unitarian Universalists
11. Choir
12. Swing dancing
13. Gay/lesbian, bisexual, and/or transgender groups
14. Forum or discussion
15. Men's group
16. Women's group
17. Bridge
18. Pagans
19. Unitarian Universalist Jewish Group
20. Bereavement Group

Your congregation may have ideas for groups. Help these groups form and meet, then consider supportive ways to make sure that people keep coming. Some groups may meet for a time and then disband; others will go on forever.

FIGHTING INFECTIONS

Every congregation, if it is to remain healthy, also needs white blood cell members. White blood cells fight infections in the body. But there is only one white blood cell for every 500 to 1,000 red blood cells in the body. In congregational life, this means that congregations have far fewer "white cell" members than "red cell" members.

"White cell" members are not only bigger than "red cell" members—sometimes they seem larger than life. They work devotedly when the going is tough. They are persistent and effective. These members are, in a sense, the keepers of morals and values in a congregation. They fight for right relationships and hang in there during conflict. They come from congregations that have evolved systems to keep healthy, using formally discussed and affirmed congregational and ministerial codes of conduct, harassment policies, child abuse prevention policies, conflict prevention resources, open communication, and ceremonies of affirmation and celebration.

WHEN A VIRUS STRIKES

Like viruses, destructive problems or conflicts appear in congregations. If undealt with, they can integrate their genetic material into the host—the congregation—and remain for generations. Viruses attack and weaken the body. Here is a list of viruses to watch out for, plus tips on fighting them off.

Twenty Viruses to Watch Out For

1. *The toxic personalities virus:* This is the person who is determinedly, chronically, relentlessly critical, mean, unhappy, or sour. No matter what you do, this person is never satisfied. If you have tried talking to the person directly, and the congregation has made its feelings known to the person and nothing changes, you may have to ask the person to leave the congregation. Talk to your minister about it.

2. *The tyranny of the minority virus:* Because Unitarian Universalists prize individual freedom, we can let people run over us. While we honor the individual's right to speak, it should never be at the cost of community health or well-being. No one has the right to speak on behalf of the whole community. No one has the right to hurt, overwhelm, or intimidate others. Sometimes a person or a small minority of persons will terrorize a congregation because (in the name of free speech) the majority is afraid to stop them. Just say, "No, I'm sorry, but that is not appropriate here. We do not function that way." This is a time when a Congregational Covenant of Good Relations, or a Congregational Conflict Management team and policy pay off.

3. *The single-issue personalities virus:* This is the person who only wants to talk about one thing. The agenda is always the same. The group must let this person know (if it is the case) that this is not the time or place for *that* agenda.

4. *The gossip versus communication virus:* One virulent congregational disease is to talk about and not to a person. There is a simple cure: Ask yourself, and/or the person who may be gossiping: "Do I have permission to say this? Is it my news to give? What good purpose would it serve to share this news?" If you don't have permission,

or it is not your news, or if sharing serves no purpose, don't say it. If the other person persists, just say, "Sorry, I'd rather not talk about that." Or "Sorry, I don't keep secrets." Or "I don't think it is up to us to share this news."

5. *The dangerous person virus:* Some people are dangerous. Whether they are sexual predators, child molesters, thieves, or stalkers, you and your board may conclude that it is not in the interest of your congregation for them to remain members. You can be prepared for these kinds of events by making sure your congregational bylaws are clear about removing people from membership.

6. *The bad mouth virus:* Beware of the person with the big bad mouth! He or she never has a kind word to say about a soul, a project, or an idea. If Jesus or the Buddha were a member of the congregation, a bad mouth would complain that the one was too hairy and the other was sneaky because he smiled a lot. Just politely say, "I'm not interested in hearing this."

7. The *"We tried that and it didn't work syndrome"* usually infects long-term members who have developed resistance to change. Try saying, "Well, if we did try it, what would it be like?" or, "Yes, I know and appreciate that you tried that (x) years ago. We're going to try it again now, and perhaps we'll have better luck than you did!" or, "There are different people in our congregation now. Perhaps things will be different. Let's try it again!"

8. *The secret group virus:* This is a cluster that meets privately and often secretly to complain about, criticize, or try to get rid of people or changes. If you are invited to join such a group or if you know of one, tell them they need to talk to the source of their complaint and not to each other about the problem. Unless they go to the source (and if that doesn't work, are willing to deal with the problem through congregational channels) nothing will change. Let them know what you think. Encourage them to be open in their work for change. Tell them you will go with them or help them find a "prudent listener" to go with them to talk to the person about whom they are concerned. If they are unwilling, talk to the minister, the board, or the Committee on Ministry to see if they can't be

helped to deal directly with their issue. But be sure to tell them, "I don't do secrets!"

9. *The defamation of character virus:* infects a person or persons who constantly criticize or put down others. Tell them to stop, that the only person they should talk to is the person they are criticizing. Say that you believe that it is unappealing to criticize other people when they are not there and that you would prefer not to listen.

10. *The rumors virus:* When people tell you a rumor, say cheerfully, "Well, let's go to the source!"; then make a date to do it. If they are unwilling, tell them you will not participate in spreading rumors and you hope they will stop, too. Tell them you are willing to go with them to check it out, but not to carry it on. If the rumor is false, make sure the person who told you knows, and ask that person to correct the rumor with everyone she or he told.

11. *The triangulation virus:* happens when Mr. A comes to talk to you about Ms. B. Mr. A is putting you in the middle. The only solution is to say, "I don't want to be put in the middle of you. If you have something to say about Ms. B, go tell her, not me." Never let yourself get put between two people who are having a disagreement. Don't take sides. The safest and most honorable course of action is to ask the two people to deal directly with each other or to seek help in dealing directly with each other.

12. *The manipulation/pressure virus:* Sometimes you may feel pressured or manipulated into doing something. Always ask yourself: "Am I doing this because I want to? Or because I feel pressured to?" If you take on tasks that you have been pressured or manipulated into doing, you will probably not enjoy or feel good about them. Choose the tasks and the work that you are interested in and want to do. Just say, "No, thanks," to all others.

13. *The ambush virus:* Occasionally, people who are new to a congregation or one of its committees may try to take it over to suit their own purposes. If you think this is happening, talk to your minister or board president right away.

14. *The blackmail virus:* Have you ever heard someone say something like, "Well if you're going to start canvassing people to pledge, I'm

quitting!" or "If you are not going to have the volunteer thank-you dinner where I suggested, I want nothing to do with it." This may be a member who has made a large pledge or contributes a great deal of work to the congregation. It is still blackmail to say to people that you will quit or leave if they don't do it your way. If the majority of the group has agreed to do something that you disagree with, support the will of the community. (Unless, of course, you believe what they are doing is illegal, harmful, or morally wrong.) If you are in a group that is being blackmailed, just respond politely, "I'm sorry you feel that way. We will miss you, and if you change your mind, we'll welcome you back."

15. *The sitting-on-the-franchise virus* (or the keep-the-status-quo virus) almost always infects only long-time members. Their position is that things are fine the way they are and they are not willing to change. Too often their attitude drives away people who are actively seeking a religious community. Try talking to them directly about the problem. Say that with growth comes change and that for people, like plants, growth is a healthy thing. If they are still unwilling to let anyone into the congregation who is not willing to do what they want, call your District Office to discuss how to resolve the problem.

16. *The money-is-ugly virus:* Some people don't want to talk about, hear about, ask for, or give money. Major medicine is needed to clear up this problem. Call in a specialist (ask your District Office) to help educate your congregation about a theology of abundance. Giving is a privilege and a responsibility, and it feels good. Congregations need money to work and pledges to plan ahead. They need community capital to stay alive. But sometimes people have to learn this—they don't automatically know it.

17. *The poor communication virus:* When people feel "out of the loop," this is your virus. Every congregation should have multiple, effective forms of communication. A good, attractive newsletter, uncluttered bulletin boards, succinct announcements, and a telephone tree are ways to ensure that the word gets out and around.

18. *The power trip virus:* One of the great lessons of history is: "Those

whom the gods would destroy, they first make mad with power." If someone in your congregation is misusing power, such as ordering the staff around without authority, making public comments on behalf of the congregation without permission, or spending money without consent, it is the responsibility of the board to stop him or her. Ask a board member to go with you to talk to the person, then let the board do its work. (See item 11, the triangulation virus.)

19. *The apathy virus:* When committees stop meeting or most members don't show up for meetings, something is wrong. Call them together and ask them what it is. If it seems that they are not interested, or the task is no longer needed, ask them if this is the work they want to be doing for the congregation. People who are not interested in or do not care about the work of a committee should resign from it.

20. *Virus X* hasn't been discovered yet. Write us and tell us about it, especially if you have discovered the cure.

These viruses are stopped in their tracks by one thing: members of the congregation paying attention and putting an end to wrong behaviors. Be a white blood cell member. Be an active red blood cell member. Keep the congregation strong, healthy, and lively.

MORE GOOD STUFF TO READ

Phillips, Roy D. *Transforming Liberal Congregations for the New Millennium.* Roy D. Phillips, 1996. Theoretical and practical answers to help revitalize liberal congregations.

Steinke, Peter L. *Healthy Congregations.* Nashville, TN: Alban Institute Publications, 1993. Helpful suggestions about nurturing church systems. Covers ten principles of health and offers healthier ways for congregations to actively promote well-being.

Ears

CHAPTER FOUR

Fostering Good Communications

Can a congregation hear? Or do its members hear? Both the congregation and the individual who speaks out and takes in, listens and hears, will be compassionate, fair, and inclusive. It has been said that to speak the truth requires at least two people—one speaking and the other listening. The person who listens must also hear; what is being said must be understood and integrated. Good hearing inspires good communication, which is necessary for a healthy congregation.

LISTENING AND HEARING EACH OTHER

Listening requires more than ears. It takes practice. You can begin this practice by observing the people you talk to. They may send signals by leaning forward, glancing at you, seeking eye contact. You can show your interest by giving them the same signals—leaning forward, making eye contact, nodding, smiling, and so on. Allow time for silence when the other person needs it; silence can build trust. Listen to the other person's context: Nationality, gender, religion, ethnicity, experience, conditioning, and feelings all influence who we are and how we communicate. Pay attention to context as carefully as you do to words.

When our ears are blocked, we don't even hear ourselves. Learning to listen unblocks hearing. By clearing out blockages, we overcome resistance to hearing ourselves and others. Openness to hearing the other begins by listening to and knowing yourself. It begins when you train yourself to listen with an unthreatening, non-evaluating, non-judgmental attitude. This openness contributes by deed and as a model to the good health of the congregation.

Here's a useful exercise to help you understand how well you listen to others.

Help!

Make it better!

Help me! Will you listen?

How can I help you?

What have I to say?

Say nothing. Be unknowing.

Dare to be silent and loving.

All you need to do is

Be there for this person:

    Imagine they are perfect

    Imagine the pain flowing

    through them

        tears are not the pain

        tears are the release

        of the pain.

Imagine them becoming whole

    again.

Imagine that you love them.

—SYDNEY MORRIS

GOOD HEARING CHECKUP

Take a quiet moment to ask yourself the following questions.

_____ Do I want to listen to this person? Do I want to get the most I can out of this conversation?

_____ Am I interested in this person? In the subject? Even if I don't start out interested, can I listen attentively for something that is useful or important?

_____ Do I tune in to this person? Or tune out? Do I bring my full attention to the conversation—employing some of the unused portion of my brain? Or does my attention drift to other things?

_____ Do I focus and concentrate on concepts the speaker is trying to share, looking for structure and major threads?

_____ Do I stay with the person, tolerating distractions, staying with the content and not framing my responses to details?

_____ Do I question, restate, repeat, paraphrase, summarize? Am I supportive, understanding, reflecting back?

_____ Do I take mental notes? Could I summarize what this person has said?

_____ Do I resist judging before the person has finished speaking? Do I wait to evaluate by not interrupting, watching for, and recognizing my own barriers and filters to good hearing?

_____ Do I control my emotional reactions? Am I aware of my deaf spots, the things I have difficulty hearing? My hot spots, things that upset me?

_____ Do I practice listening? Am I always aware of my need to improve?

Hearing improves with practice. Try taking this Good Hearing Checkup to committee members, to a board retreat, or to a congregational support or affinity group one evening. After you've finished, discuss the results.

LISTENING TRIADS

The following exercise is a good activity for your committee members, board, or congregation to try after completing the Good Hearing Checkup. As the facilitator (also the timekeeper), divide everyone into groups of three—preferably with people they know less well. Offer a subject like, "How do you feel when you are faced with conflict?" (or choose an ethical or religious theme) for discussion, such as the right to die. Ask each group to identify one person as A, one as B, and one as C. Make sure everyone understands the following guidelines:

Participant A begins as speaker, B as listener, and C as observer. The participants rotate the three positions about every seven minutes, until each participant has had a turn in each position. The discussion should be unstructured except that before each participant speaks, he or she must first summarize in his or her own words what has been said previously. If the summary is incorrect, the speaker or observer should interrupt and clear up misunderstandings.

The observer answers these questions after each session: Was the speaker being heard? Was the listener reflecting accurately? Afterwards, invite the whole group to discuss these questions:

- If you had difficulty listening to the others during the exercise, why? (Look back at the Good Hearing Checkup.)
- Did you have difficulty formulating your thoughts and listening at the same time?
- When others paraphrased your comments, did they do it in a more concise way? Did they add their own slant?
- Did you find you were not getting across what you wanted to say?
- Did anything the others said or did affect your listening skills?

THE ZEN MASTER AND THE SCHOLAR

Ted Tollefson, Unitarian Universalist community minister, tells this old Buddhist story in the Mythos Institute newsletter, *Synergy*. The original story can be found in *Zen Flesh/Zen Bones* by Paul Reps.

Perhaps you are familiar with the story of the scholar and the Zen master meeting over a cup of tea. The Zen master asks the scholar what he knows about Zen. The scholar, needing no further invitation, eagerly reels off pages of comments, literary allusions, footnotes, and portions of old lectures.

As the scholar talks and talks, the Zen master pours the tea without stopping. Finally, when the legs and feet of the scholar are thoroughly soaked, he follows the trail of tea back to the gentle, smiling face of the Zen master. "What are you doing? Why do you continue to pour when my cup is full to overflowing?" asks the scholar with some indignation.

"How can I teach you anything about Zen," says the Zen master, "until you first empty your cup?"

Being a good listener, one who hears, requires emptying our cups.

- Clear your mind of all thoughts and concerns.
- Listen to the content of what the speaker is saying.
- Try not to make judgments as you listen.
- Wait to hear what is actually being said.
- Actively listen—reflect back to the speaker and make sure you understand.
- Listen to the facts and the feelings of the speaker.
- Lean forward.
- Pay respectful and close attention.

PRACTICE IN ACTIVE LISTENING

You can do this exercise with a friend. You can also gather together pairs of people from the congregation who will first meet together to learn the process, then do 12 weeks in pairs, and finally gather again at the end of the 12 weeks to discuss and evaluate the process. The group may then decide to continue with the same pairs, new partners, and/or different topics—or they may decide not to continue.

Here is the process: pair up with someone whom you like and trust. Agree to actively listen to one another for two hours a week, every week for 12 weeks.

You do not problem solve—your role is to actively listen to your partner for one hour; for one hour he or she actively listens to you.

You do not judge or offer solutions. You just listen, attentively, compassionately, fully. You should discuss boundaries and agree to complete confidentiality.

Each of you may talk about any topic you want. One interesting progression is to learn about each other's life. The following 12 life topics are possibilities. You may wish to develop a list of your own.

- childhood
- my mother
- my father
- adolescence
- adulthood
- what being a woman or man means for me
- people I have loved
- my spiritual/religious journey
- work and my work history
- my best friends
- where I want to be in ten years
- old age and dying

"Words are very heavy magic."

—STEPHEN

Always listen carefully to the other person. Learn who he or she is, how beautiful, how caring, how loving, how broken, how whole, how healthy, how kind, how singular and special. Trust the person to learn about you.

Listen carefully to yourself. Learn who you are, how beautiful, how caring, how loving, how broken, how whole, how healthy, how kind, how singular and special.

To have the courage to include, one must overcome the fear of rejection and become vulnerable. Hear the other by listening to yourself.

LISTENING AND HEARING IN SMALL GROUPS

Small groups, like committees, are rewarding and challenging. One of the rewards is experiencing the accomplishments of shared work. Sometimes small group communications get stuck in dissension or inactivity.

There are many causes for bad communication in congregational groups. And there are ways to keep the air clean and the lines of communication flowing. People block information and communication for many reasons. We may have been having a bad day when the information was passed out. We may have missed the previous meeting. Perhaps someone gave us incorrect information or too much information. Check with the people who feel they are not being communicated with to be sure they have the correct information.

If we have the facts right, we can try looking over the following possibilities and see if any fits. People tend to skip over details or feel uninformed or unheard when they confront obstacles, such as:

- The purpose, mission, or task of the committee or group is unclear.
- The boundaries of the committee are unclear; there may be two or three committees trying to do the same work.
- When people are not involved in the planning or the decision making and do not understand how the outcome will affect them
- When there is poor communication and they were not informed
- When there is a loss of power or "face"
- When there is a fear of failure
- When they are personally anxious about the outcome
- When there is lack of trust in, or respect for one person, or several persons in the group
- When they are happy with the status quo and don't want to hear about changes.

TRUST BUILDING

To improve communication within your congregational groups, begin by building trust. Use one meeting for a discussion of the group's process. Have a moment of attention and silence each time you begin a group meeting. Get centered. Be present. Together, try some of the listening exercises described in the previous section. Ask: "How well do I listen and hear?" Next, discuss: How does our group make decisions? If not everyone has spoken and not everyone has been heard, are decisions being made by the whole group? Develop ground rules for good communication, such as:

- Agree to begin and end on time, so people won't feel pressed.
- Everyone will have a chance to speak once before anyone speaks twice.
- Alternate pro and con speakers on any given issue. Have someone record on butcher paper on the wall what is being said. That way there is a group memory that is clearly documented and everyone can agree that it accurately reflects what was said.
- Try not to speak in code—don't assume everyone knows everything.
- Take breaks at long meetings.
- Have job descriptions for the committee and members.
- Have timed agendas and stick to them.
- What would you like to happen so that the group feels trust in the group process? What will happen if trust breaks down?

Talk. Listen. Repeat back. Ask. Check things out. Repeat until you get it right. Leave spaces in the conversation. Conversation is a work in progress that more than one person constructs.

INTRACONGREGATIONAL HEARING

Ask yourselves the following question: Do we as a congregation really listen to each other? How well do we communicate? In other words, how is our intracongregational hearing?

To find out, get conscious. Organize intentional, formal ways to communicate. Make sure you have strong formal systems for getting the word out, such as a newsletter that is readable, attractive, and regular, an uncluttered bulletin board or kiosk, pew cards, and a telephone tree.

Hold large- and small-group meetings. Is the democratic process alive and healthy in your congregation? These meetings should be open,

"It's the holes in space that make the lace!"

—SAYING AROUND STARR KING SCHOOL, MID-1970S

well-advertised, and planned in advance. There should be a clearly defined and pre-announced agenda and guidelines for good relationship and ethical behavior in the meetings.

Make sure your Committee on Ministry is working and strong. This committee should have its fingers on the pulse of the congregation and know when congregational life is strong or weak. Make sure committee members let the congregation know that they are there by printing articles in the church newsletter, using special name tags that say "Committee on Ministry," or doing a service one Sunday a year.

Take advantage of other formal and informal opportunities to communicate, such as holding a coffee hour, printing announcements in the order of service, sending out interesting postcards as invitations to special meetings, posting flyers in the building, and using email and creating a Web page. You can also designate topic tables at pot lucks.

Congregations with good ears listen and talk to one another regularly and with respect in a multitude of ways.

MORE GOOD STUFF TO READ

Moore, Donna J. *Up Close and Personal: Experiential Exercises for Building a Spiritual Community*. Bainbridge Island, WA: Unitarian Universalist Fellowship of Bainbridge Island and North Kitsap, 1997. Designed for lay leaders who want to conduct adult interactive exercises within their congregations.

Eyes

CHAPTER FIVE

Developing a Congregational Future

Imagine all sorts of eyes: bloodshot eyes, bedroom eyes, shifty eyes, soulful eyes, black eyes, smoldering eyes. Imagine what it might be like to be blind, or color blind. What adaptations would be necessary?

What might it be like to have eyes that are always out of focus? What happens when your vision is blurred? Look around and notice how your eyes adjust between near and far distances in vision. When do you know that you need corrective lenses? Four-fifths of our learning comes through our eyes or is decoded by them. What adaptations do we make when we don't see clearly? Our eyes send messages to other people about what we think and feel and how and who we are. Other people learn about who we are from what they read in our eyes. It has been said that the eyes are the windows of the soul.

In such a way, congregational eyes are a window to the issues of body, mind, and spirit that draw us together as a community. Our congregational eyes are a measure of our vision and our personal well-being. They reflect our activities, passion, vitality, and heart, as well as our sense of ministry. Just as it is hard to disguise the condition of the eyes, it is hard to disguise a congregation without a vision or a mission.

Sometimes mission and vision are confused with other important congregational matters like covenant and values. The following definitions and exercises will clarify the differences among values, covenant, vision, and mission. A congregation that takes the time to explore, identify, and commit to them will become focused and purposeful.

CONGREGATIONAL VALUES

Every congregation has values it holds dear that represent the ways of being together and in the world that the congregation has (consciously or unconsciously) agreed on. It is healthiest to agree upon these values together and publicly commit to them.

In *Values and Teaching*, Sid Simon writes that valuing is "not concerned with the *content* of people's values, but the process of valuing. [Louis Raths'] focus is on how people come to hold certain beliefs and establish certain behavior patterns." Valuing, according to Raths, includes seven subprocesses:

Prizing one's beliefs and behaviors
1. prizing and cherishing
2. publicly affirming, when appropriate

Choosing one's beliefs and behaviors
3. choosing from alternatives
4. choosing after consideration of consequences
5. choosing freely

Acting on one's beliefs
6. acting
7. acting with a pattern, consistency, and repetition.

Try the following workshop to determine what your congregation values.

VALUES WORKSHOP

One hour and 40 minutes.

These exercises are presented in a particular order. If you have a values Sunday, or a values workshop, try to use the exercises in this order: 1) exploring what values mean; 2) what do we value?; and 3) what do we *really* value?

Exploring What Values Mean (30 minutes)
Discuss the definition of values and make sure everybody understands it. Post and explain Sid Simon and Lois Raths's definition of values. Everyone should

> *"Where there is no vision, the people perish."*
>
> —PROVERBS

understand that although our values may be different, that is all right.

For instance, freedom of choice and the right to life are both intrinsically worthwhile values. Troubles arise when they begin to conflict, as in the issue of abortion. It is because they conflict with each other that the abortion debate rages on. It is only when people are unwilling to hear, or to recognize the depth and worth of another person's values, that troubles and conflict begin. Ask people to start with a willingness to hear.

What Do We Value?   (30 minutes)

Ask the group, "Does everyone know what a brainstorm is? A brainstorm is a list generated by everyone in the group. The ground rules are that anything goes and that no one comments, argues about, or criticizes what goes on the list. We keep adding things until we run out of ideas or time.

"Let's practice first. Why don't we brainstorm how many ways there are to get into a bathtub." (*Brainstorm for a maximum of five minutes.*)

"Now let's brainstorm our values. What do we—as individuals—prize and cherish? Remember the values we list can be positive, negative, and/or neutral!" (*Continue the brainstorm until the group slows down.*)

What Do We Really Value?   (30 minutes)

Pass out three dots to each participant. Say, "You each have three dots. In a few minutes, after you have carefully studied our brainstormed list, I will signal to you to get up and place your dots on the three values that you feel are the most important for this congregation. Vote for three different values, rather than placing all your dots on one." (*Wait one minute.*)

"Let's put the dots on now." (*Give the group five minutes.*)

"Let's count the dots. (*With different colored pens, count and record the number of dots next to each value.*) What can we learn from this? Which ten values are most important to this congregation?" (*On a clean piece of paper, make a top ten list.*)

"That was great work. (*Lead applause.*) Now that we know what our congregational values are, we can see if they are consistent with our current covenant or if we want to change it." (*If the congregation does not have a covenant, say: ". . . now we can write a covenant."*)

Newsprint

Butcher paper

Marking pens in different colors

Masking tape

Adhesive dots

Chalice or candle

Recording of "El Condor Pasa" by Simon and Garfunkel and a cassette tape player

Find a room with plenty of wall or window space. Put the butcher paper up on the wall or window in advance. Make sure everyone sits so they can see the butcher paper. On newsprint, print out Sid Simon and Louis Raths's definition of values.

Closing   (10 minutes)

Light a chalice or a candle. Play or have someone sing "El Condor Pasa" by Simon and Garfunkel. Read out loud at five-second intervals the ten values most dear to this group. Finally, say, "May we hold these values in our hearts; may they shine from our eyes and our deeds. May the world know who we are by the way we live these values day by day. Go in peace."

CONGREGATIONAL COVENANT

"Love is the spirit of this church."

—JAMES VILLA BLAKE

A covenant is *about* values, what the congregation most highly values and the promises it makes together about how its members will act with one another. A covenant says to the world, "Here are our highest values. This is who we are together as a religious liberal community." A covenant is often a regular part of the Sunday service, spoken in unison by all members of a congregation.

If your congregation does not have a covenant, plan to do the Values Workshop from the previous section. At the end of the workshop, gather together a small (five-person) task force to draft a covenant, using the (no more than) ten values the group identified as the content. Let the task force create the poetic form.

Try out two or three versions, each on a different Sunday morning, including them in the order of service as unison readings. Ask for people's comments and preferences, with the understanding that the Covenant Task Force will not change the basic list of values and may not be able to incorporate every suggestion. The final draft should be pleasing and poetic, expressing the soul that shines from your congregational eyes.

When one final draft is written, submit it to a congregational vote. Vote yes or no, up or down, no amendments. If at least 75 percent of the congregation votes yes, you have a covenant. This vote may be taken at a congregational meeting or by mail.

The Sunday after the vote, have the entire congregation sing: "Gathered Here in the Mystery of the Hour" (hymn #389) or "Here We Have Gathered" (hymn #360) from *Singing the Living Tradition.* Then join in a unison reading of the new covenant. From then on, print it with your mission on the order of service and in the congregational brochure. Recite it together each Sunday.

CONGREGATIONAL VISION

A vision statement answers the question: "What are our dreams? What do we want this congregation to look like in five years?" It includes specific, measurable objectives, achievable in a prescribed amount of time. For example: "We envision that the East Cupcake Unitarian Universalist Congregation will serve 250 adults and 125 children by the year 2000. We envision our buildings to be accessible to wheelchairs on all floors of our building, that we will serve the diversity of our town as proactively as we can, that we will have seven affinity groups that will meet monthly, that we will move to two Sunday morning services as we prepare for a larger building and the capital campaign that it requires. We envision hiring a half-time professional religious educator and a half-time church coordinator in addition to our minister."

A vision statement makes real plans from dreams—for the congregation's future. Here's a workshop that will help your congregation define and develop its vision.

VISION WORKSHOP

Make sure that everyone in the congregation is not only invited but urged to attend. Provide child care so that all parents may participate. The more people involved, the truer your vision will be.

Opening Worship   (10 minutes)

Use a reading such as #453, "Passover Haggadah," or #448, "We Gather this Hour . . . ," in *Singing the Living Tradition*. Light the chalice and invite everyone to look around the room at the people gathered, those they know and those they know less well. Ask them to speak the new or renewed covenant in unison, and then to sing hymn #389, "Gathered Here."

Close with the words: "We are a tribe, a clan, on an important life journey. As we have journeyed together through the years of this congregation's life, so may we journey together, joyfully, passionately, courageously, lovingly into our future."

Name tags

Adhesive dots in
different colors

Butcher paper or newsprint

Water-based marking pens

Masking tape

Cassette player or
sound system

There should be sufficient space
for people to break into small
groups so everyone can be
heard. People will be dividing
into groups of eight based on
the colored dots on their
name tags. Prepare name tags
by using a different-colored
dot for every set of eight
participants.

Guided Meditation   **(15+ minutes)**

You may prefer not to use music, but if you do, choose a soft, pleasing piece of music for the tape recorder. Classical music that is fluid and soft is good. Do not use music with words or voices. Be sure the tape will last at least a half hour, uninterrupted. Be sure to fade the music in and out at the beginning and the end, as the abrupt sound of a stop button can be jarring.

Practice reading the following guided meditation out loud, not too slowly and not too fast. Be sure you are familiar with the words.

"Please make yourself comfortable. Put both feet on the floor. Shut your eyes." (*Fade in music.*)

"Relax. Take deep easy breaths, inhaling and exhaling slowly. Follow your natural breath." (*15 seconds of silence.*)

"Imagine yourself in your own home, in your own bed, awakening on a Sunday morning. . . . It is a beautiful day, the sky is clear and deep blue. . . . You stretch, go to open a window and breathe the fresh, cool air. . . . (*15 seconds of silence.*)

"It is Sunday and it is five years in the future. You are in the best future you can imagine for your congregation. You smile, because you look forward to being with your community of friends this morning. You get a bite to eat, a cup of coffee or tea, aromatic and awakening, and then you leave the house and get in your car. If you have a family, imagine them with you, happy, talking, ready to go. (*10 seconds of silence.*)

"You drive along the familiar roads, relishing the spring day, noticing how beautiful it is, how bright the flowers, how green the leaves and grass. . . . (*10 seconds of silence.*)

"You arrive at church. Where do you park? Do you feel safe walking to the building? Is it the building you have now, or a different, new one? Are there trees and flowers around the building?" (*10 seconds of silence.*)

"You look at the building with affection and pride. You notice your friends entering the wide open doors. Are there many people you don't know? New people? Or the same familiar faces? Some of each? Are people pouring in, standing and talking, or both? Is the entrance welcome and inviting? What does it look like?" (*10 seconds of silence.*)

"Children rush to greet friends. You go into the meeting house. Does your family all go together, or have the children gone to a different space?" (*Five seconds of silence.*)

"Tell me of thine eyes
And I will tell thee of thy heart."

—FROM *DUNE* BY FRANK HERBERT

"You look in at the meeting space. What does it look like? Is it the same? Are there windows? What can you see out of them? Do you sit in chairs or pews? How many people does the room hold? Is there an organ or piano playing?" (*Five seconds of silence.*)

"You go out and then go into the office, passing other spaces. Is it just the same as it is now? If not, how is it different? Is there more space, or is the space more crowded? What is the religious education space like? Is it attractive? Child centered?

"You wave at the children and leave. If you do not have children, you notice how the children are and where they go. Perhaps you smile and wave at some you know." (*Five seconds of silence.*)

"You move back into the sanctuary again. It is almost time for the service to begin. Is the sanctuary full? Crowded? Empty? The prelude begins. You look around and smile at faces you know and love. The music swells, the voices rise, the words come forth to challenge your mind and move your heart." (*10 seconds of silence.*)

"After the service you look at the bulletin boards, the walls, the literature rack. What is your congregation doing now? Same or different things or some of each? You get a cup of coffee and talk to friends. You converse with a newcomer who tells you why he or she likes it here. You smile and agree. What did that person say to you?" (*15 seconds of silence.*)

"Now, please allow yourself to remember this morning and our congregation of the future. Then return your attention to this room and the people in it with whom you will share your vision." (*Five seconds of silence.*)

"Now, as you are ready, open your eyes."

After 30 seconds or so, fade out music and invite people to return to the present. Wait for all the eyes to open and for people to focus on you.

Sharing Individual Visions   (45 minutes)

Announce, "Soon we will divide into small groups. First, I would like to give you instructions. In each group, you will need to identify one person to be the recorder and then report back to the large group. Here are the paper and marking pens. You will have 45 minutes to discuss your vision and to identify the common elements in all your visions.

"First, go around the circle and let each person briefly describe their 'church of the future' and then talk about what you all share, and what you liked,

"open mine eyes that I may see . . ."

—OLD PROTESTANT HYMN

but did not think of that other people may have mentioned. This process should be consensual, which means that everyone in the group can live with the final results but not every person has to agree with every item on every other person's list.

"Each group should bring back one sheet of paper with their vision. Are there any questions?"

Have participants divide into groups of eight based on the colored dots on their name tags.

Building a Vision   (30 minutes)

After a brief break, when everyone has returned to the large group ask each small group's recorder to report on their group vision. Post each report on the wall. Have everyone spend a few minutes studying the lists.

Ask for feedback and record it on newsprint: "Which items appear the most frequently? Are there commonalties or affinities, or groupings that you notice? Is anything missing?"

Do a values voting. Ask people to vote—each person gets three votes, or uses dots—for those things on the group list that they think have the highest priority for this congregation. These priorities will become the foundation of the congregational vision. Ask for a volunteer from each group to form a task force to write up the vision and post it on the social hall wall and put it in the newsletter. Or have a Vision Sunday, when the material is presented to everyone in the congregation.

Closing   (5 minutes)

Ask people to join in a circle. Play Louis Armstrong's "It's a Wonderful World," music by The Gypsy Kings, Judy Collins's "Open the Door," or another equally upbeat piece of music. Invite them to move around and shake hands or trade hugs on their accomplishment, their wonderful dream for the future of the congregation. To keep the music going throughout, you may need to make a tape with several songs.

MISSION STATEMENTS

A mission statement naturally follows the accomplishments of covenant and vision. A mission statement expresses the mission of the congregation in a memorable way that is brief and to the point. For example,

Olympia Unitarian Universalist Congregation inspires lives of passion, compassion, and community.

> We nourish spirituality, intellectual growth, and our ties to one another.
> We do this for ourselves and for the larger world.

—Olympia Unitarian Universalist Congregation, Olympia, Washington

Our purpose is to build a compassionate faith community which is multicultural in membership and celebration and which works for justice in our neighborhoods, our city, and the larger world.

—The Rainier Valley Unitarian Universalist Congregation, Seattle, Washington

The Pacific Northwest District Board will increase Unitarian Universalist presence in the Pacific Northwest, and will enhance the development of member congregations.

—The Pacific Northwest District of the Unitarian Universalist Association

"This little light of mine, I'm gonna let it shine!"

— HYMN #118,

SINGING THE LIVING TRADITION

A mission statement says who we are and what we value. It says, given who we are, here is our social contract and this is how we will make congregational life more meaningful. It uses active rather than passive verbs and clearly states what good we want to do in the world and with whom. Remember, a mission statement is a living document that should be reviewed periodically.

A congregation's mission, deeply felt, shines out of its members' eyes. It informs their work as a religious community so that members of the congregation—and the larger community—know who they are and what they stand for. A congregation that cares only about itself may need corrective lenses so that it will see farther than its own walls.

MISSION STATEMENT WORKSHOP

A mission statement workshop should be preceded by congregational work on values, covenant, and vision. When you have accomplished this work, you will know the values you share and the future you wish to achieve. Developing a mission statement flows naturally from this work and gives a congregation a sense of solidarity, purpose, and common ground.

Three hours.

Name tags on a check-in table

Sign-in sheet

Butcher paper or newsprint

Marking pens in different colors

Masking tape

3" x 5" cards for each person

Tape player and music cassettes

The room you are meeting in will need plenty of light and wall space. The committee members should arrive early to make sure the lights and heat are on and that the chairs and tables are set up properly. If possible, have six to eight chairs around each table—participants will need to write and work in small groups. Have music playing as people enter; have flowers or greenery on each table; and have a chalice and a bell.

Before starting this workshop, ask the board to appoint a Mission Workshop Day Planning Committee. Make sure the members represent the diversity of the congregation—parents, elders, singles, with ranges of belief, and so on. The committee and the board should decide how they wish to identify a facilitator. It is best to use an outside facilitator so that every member of the congregation can participate and to ensure that the facilitator is neutral. Prospects for facilitators are: your District Executive, district or congregational consultants, a facilitator from a neighboring congregation—offer a trade, or a local professional facilitator.

If the facilitator has not worked with this process before, meet with the facilitator to share what you wish to do—to create a congregational mission statement for the next three to five years. Share the suggested process with him or her. It may be used, adapted, or substituted with an entirely different process. However, for a mission statement to be adopted by a congregation it should receive no less than a 75 percent vote at a congregational meeting.

To arrive at a successful mission statement, it is important to involve every member of the congregation. Every member of the congregation should be personally invited to attend with a letter of invitation and by telephone. Committee and board members can divide up the membership list and make the calls. The Mission Statement Workshop should be publicized with child care provided so all parents can attend. Make sure the child-care provider is not a member of the congregation.

Depending on the time of the workshop, you may wish to provide food paid for by the congregation and cooked (and cleaned up afterwards) by non-members. Often a neighboring congregation will do this as a trade—they'll bring in the food, prepare it and serve it, and clean up.

Opening

Have music playing as people arrive. When it is time to begin, fade out the music. Invite people into silence to think about why this congregation is in the world. Read the definitions of a covenant, a vision, and a mission statement. Tell them that what they are here to do today is honorable and important work.

Read Marge Piercy's poem, "To Be of Use" (#567 in *Singing the Living Tradition*). Let a few moments of silence pass after you have finished. Then ring a bell or chime and say: "Now let us begin this work, which is real."

Drafting Statements   (90 minutes)

Say to the group, "I'd like to read you the definition of a mission statement and some examples of mission statements from other congregations." (*Read these documents aloud.*)

"After a minute of silence, during which you imagine a mission for your congregation, please take your 3" x 5" card and write your best effort at a mission statement for our congregation on the card. Mission statements should be brief, crisp, and to the point. One ought to be able to remember it easily, so that if someone were to ask you what the mission of your congregation was, you could tell them clearly. Please do this work in silence and do not compare notes with your neighbors. (*Wait five minutes.*)

"Is everyone done? Now, in a moment, please stand up. But first, look around. I would like you to find a person in the room you do not know particularly well and then pull two chairs together and sit down. Begin by taking turns sharing your mission statements with each other and explaining why you believe your mission statement would work for our congregation.

"Next, by consensus, each pair should come up with one mission statement between you. Consensus means that while it may not be a perfect match, you can both live with it. You will have 15 minutes to do this." (*Wait 15 minutes, but give a five-minute warning.*)

"Ready? Now would each pair join up with another pair, making groups of four, and repeat the process. You will need to end up with one statement for your quartet. You have 20 minutes to do this." (*Wait 20 minutes, giving a five-minute warning.*)

"Okay. Let's have each quartet find another quartet, forming groups of eight, and repeat the process. When you are done, write your group statement on newsprint in big, readable letters, and have someone present it to the whole group. You have 30 minutes." (*Give warnings at 15 and five minutes.*)

Comparing Statements

Invite each group to post and to read its statements. Invite the large group to comment on similarities and differences between the statements.

"What the eye can't see, the heart can't grieve . . ."

—ANONYMOUS

Task Force

Ask each group to meet briefly and appoint one person to be part of a task force that will combine all the statements and come up by consensus with one mission statement to propose to the whole congregation. Ask those people to meet with you briefly after the workshop to choose a meeting date.

The task force can be introduced at the next service, wearing bright name tags.

Closing

Play celebrative music (The Gypsy Kings), and invite everyone to hug and cheer.

Follow-up

The task force should meet as many times as necessary to complete the congregational mission statement.

Mail the proposed mission statement to every member of the congregation, accompanied by a letter explaining that at the congregational meeting (state the date) a vote will be taken to adopt the mission statement. Include the names of the people on the task force and invite responses.

To obtain maximum input, the task force invites comments, with the understanding that if only one or two people suggest serious changes, they will probably not be incorporated, but if a significant number of members suggest changes, the task force will incorporate them.

Make it clear that at the congregational meeting no amendments will be allowed and a 75 percent vote will be required for adoption.

The proposed mission statement should be printed in the newsletter and posted on church bulletin boards or on a handsomely printed piece of newsprint and posted in the foyer.

The task force should meet to discuss comments and suggestions and make changes they feel appropriate. The final result should be printed in the newsletter and read from the pulpit before the congregational meeting. At the congregational meeting, the vote is taken. If the vote fails, the board will need to decide whether to repeat the process in a year or to have a series of meetings to discuss changes.

Celebration

Once voted in, the new mission statement should be printed everywhere: in the order of service, stationery, congregational brochures, board manuals, and on pieces of bright paper so that every committee can have one. Post it on all bulletin boards, too.

When you know your values, covenant, vision, and mission, your congregational eyes should be clear and far-seeing. The clearer your eyes and your vision, the clearer the channels will be to the other parts of the congregational body. The eyes do not generate information or have ideas. They facilitate the flow of information from the external world to and from your body.

SEEING IS BELIEVING: WORKSHOP WARM-UPS

Choose one of these eye games as an ice-breaker at one of your workshops.

THE EYE CHART

Ask for a volunteer from the back of the room to read the letters on the following eye chart. Next ask everyone to warm up their eyes—who knows what the chart really says? Tell them that mission work is like this eye chart: One has to be able to see far and understand.

MAKE A MOBIUS STRIP

When does the inside become the outside and how can you tell? What is reality, anyway?

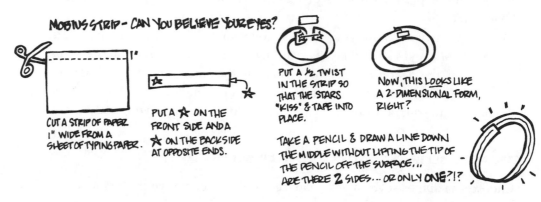

MOBIUS STRIP - CAN YOU BELIEVE YOUR EYES?

CUT A STRIP OF PAPER 1" WIDE FROM A SHEET OF TYPING PAPER.

PUT A ★ ON THE FRONT SIDE AND A ★ ON THE BACKSIDE AT OPPOSITE ENDS.

PUT A ½ TWIST IN THE STRIP SO THAT THE STARS "KISS" & TAPE INTO PLACE.

NOW, THIS LOOKS LIKE A 2-DIMENSIONAL FORM, RIGHT?

TAKE A PENCIL & DRAW A LINE DOWN THE MIDDLE WITHOUT LIFTING THE TIP OF THE PENCIL OFF THE SURFACE... ARE THERE **2** SIDES... OR ONLY **ONE**?!?

GOD'S EYE

How does magic work? What do we see with our own God's eyes? Talk about it.

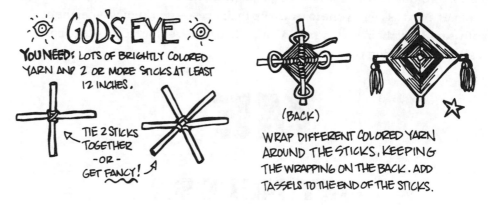

GOD'S EYE

YOU NEED: LOTS OF BRIGHTLY COLORED YARN AND 2 OR MORE STICKS AT LEAST 12 INCHES.

TIE 2 STICKS TOGETHER -OR- GET FANCY!

(BACK)

WRAP DIFFERENT COLORED YARN AROUND THE STICKS, KEEPING THE WRAPPING ON THE BACK. ADD TASSELS TO THE END OF THE STICKS.

A HUNDRED-INCH HIKE

Pair people up and give them a paper and a pencil. Send them outside and ask them to walk one hundred inches and record everything they see on the hike. Did anyone travel next to the ground? Look up? How is the seeing different, depending on perspective?

Vision and mission, like the eyes, are both a way of seeing the world and of letting the world see us—who we are and what we believe, deep in our congregational soul.

MORE GOOD STUFF TO READ

Chulak, Tom, and John Morgan. *Mission/Covenant: A Congregational Enhancement Publication.* Boston: Unitarian Universalist Association, 1987. How to develop and focus the mission and covenant of a congregation.

Simon, Sidney B., Leland W. Howe, and Howard Kirschenbaum. *Values Clarification: A Handbook of Practical Strategies for Teachers and Students.* New York: Hart Publishing Company, 1972.

Unitarian Universalist Association. *Singing the Living Tradition.* Boston: Unitarian Universalist Association, 1993. The newest hymnal, a rich source of music and readings.

Feet

CHAPTER SIX

Public Relations and Evangelism

This chapter is about letting the larger community—your town or city—know where you are, who you are, and what you are about. It's about spreading the good news. Every congregation needs to be connected to the world beyond its doors. Most of us want our community to think well of us. Ideally, we want them to say, "that Unitarian Universalist congregation is important to our town."

Being known in the community, village, town, or city opens your doors to those who are searching for a faith community, a welcoming and nurturing place to worship. They are seeking a community that shares their values, a friendly, like-minded community that cherishes freedom of thought and encourages individual spiritual growth.

How do we get known and get to know our community? There is a hint in the following story.

There was once an old wrangler named Bud who worked with a pack train. One day, mules loaded, just before riding out onto the trail, Bud whacked the lead mule hard. "First, you gotta get their attention," he muttered. Later, while off-loading the mules, Bud held forth on their various personalities and peculiarities. "That one there, she has a good sweet nature," he said, pointing. "But *that* one, you got to watch her every minute. She don't kick often, but she never misses."

Here, in a nutshell, you have two great lessons of making yourself known in the larger community: First, you gotta get their attention. Second, don't kick often, but never miss!

Being a valuable and respected presence in a town or city requires a strong sense of mission and vision. It means knowing and caring about who you are and about your town. Finally, it means having the commitment and passion to move your good work beyond the comfortable walls of your building.

Hopefully, you have identified your mission and vision. If you have not, you can consult Chapter 5, "Eyes: Developing a Congregational Future." Your next step is to find out more about yourselves and how you are experienced by the larger community. Here are some exercises to help.

WHO ARE WE AS A CONGREGATION?

This three-part exercise can accomodate very large, medium-sized, or small groups, but everyone in the congregation who can should join the process.

CONGREGATIONAL INVENTORY

The first step is to identify your congregation's values, service to the community, and mission.

Our History   (20 minutes)
Put the butcher paper on the wall. Place a stool nearby, with a bucket full of the markers. Draw a vertical line down the middle of the paper, printing PAST on the left side and PRESENT on the right side. Invite everyone to write their past and present involvement in organizations, concerns, or causes outside the congregation.

Identifying Congregational Values   (20 minutes)
Invite the group to identify the values associated with these activities and ask which values are most frequently represented. Write these core values on a new piece of newsprint and post it on the wall by the butcher paper.

How We Serve the Community   (20 minutes)
Using two sheets of newsprint, ask the group to identify the *past* (first sheet) and the *present* (second sheet) ways the congregation participates in the life of or serves the needs of the community. How has the minister been involved, if at all? Staff? What

90 minutes

4' x 8' piece of butcher paper

Many colors of marking pens

Masking tape

Newsprint

about life span learning courses? Leadership development? Social responsibility? How has the congregation as a group chosen to be involved, if at all?

Exploring Our Mission   (30 minutes)

Place a piece of paper with the words of your congregational mission on the wall. Ask the group: Is the work of our members, congregation, and leadership consistent with the mission of our congregation? Are we doing work in the community *that lives out and expresses our mission to the larger world?*

Your congregation may not wish to be involved in the community. Some congregations (known as sanctuary churches) focus inwardly on congregational community and spiritual practice.

Your congregation may be uninvolved in the community, or only marginally, but may wish to be more involved. You can brainstorm a list of ways to begin involvement. If you don't know how to begin, try doing a community exploration and assessment as outlined in Chapter 7, *Hands: Social Action and Spiritual Growth.* You can also call your District Office about a social justice workshop.

If your congregation is involved and you have identified the activities and values it represents, you are ready to begin developing a congregational profile. This is what you will let the world know about your church.

WRITING A CREATIVE BRIEF

Public relations firms and advertising agencies prepare a creative brief with their clients. It helps them understand and synthesize who the client is, identify the purpose of communications, and figure out the audience for the client's message. Congregations would profit by following this model and preparing a creative brief before they produce materials or send messages to the community. The first step is to appoint a think tank consisting of the minister, the newsletter editor, the membership chair, one or two board members, and a few creative members of the congregation of varying ages, length of membership, and perspectives. If they have experience in newsmaking or public relations, so much the better.

Distribute the following form to each of these people and ask them to bring their completed form to a meeting to discuss and consolidate the results.

(Be sure to include a copy of the mission statement and covenant with the forms.) You might also wish to distribute the form to leaders in the congregation, explaining its purpose in an accompanying letter.

Creative Brief Outline: Respond to the following questions as briefly and clearly as possible.

- Who is the primary target audience for our publications? Our membership? If also for people outside membership, who might they be? List the assumptions you make about this audience.
- What are our objectives in producing publications or news stories?
- What is the key message we wish to get across about our congregation in our publications?
- If our congregation were a product, how would you describe the character of its brand? Make up a slogan.
- What are your creative requirements—that is, what would you want the aesthetic aspects of our materials to look like?
- What is our project strategy—that is, how will we distribute or circulate these pieces, and to whom? Are they for long- or short-term use? If both, which strategies are which?
- What is the one single impression you want our materials to project?
- What convincing points can we offer to support our message?
- What is the one "call to action" you want to have come across?

Finally, convene a meeting of the think tank, with plenty of butcher paper, markers, and tape. Go through each subject heading, one by one, and from the feedback, create a unified group response to each topic. This step will probably take a series of meetings or one full day.

Once the think tank has completed this work, type it up. Mail it to the members of the group to review. Meet one more time, reviewing the results for punch and clarity. Let it become part of your publications and news-making style manual. Have this group also develop a logo. Choose paper and color(s) of ink that will be used in all congregational publications. If this group doesn't have the ability to do these steps, have them supervise an outside designer.

Here are tips for developing public relations for your congregation.

- *Consult the creative brief.* Be sure those who represent the congregation are familiar with it and comfortable speaking, writing, and representing the congregation. You may wish to identify a speakers bureau of congregational members who can represent your congregation to the public.
- *Use your logo on everything,* including press releases. Talk about how you will present your congregation, to whom, and what news stories you might write.
- *Make friends with the media.* Have one or two members (preferably someone who knows the media or who is in the business) develop a relationship with the religion editor of the local newspaper; make a contact list for other regional news organizations, newspapers, and public access television; and learn prices and rules for advertising.
- *Read the daily, weekly, and local newspapers.* Identify where you can get free coverage, such as employer newsletters, radio, public radio, public TV, theater programs, bulletin boards in bookstores, community centers, colleges, universities, and coffeehouses.
- *Identify target community organizations with which you have an affinity,* such as interfaith organizations, other religious groups, environmental groups, community beautification groups, non-profit organizations such as schools and service organizations. Post flyers or brochures on their bulletin boards.
- *Be the place for people to come to.* You can offer your building for: voting, community forums, candidates night or debates, concerts, dances, art shows and art fairs, rummage sales and flea markets, book sales and a bookstore, math camp, study hall for after-school tutoring, nursery school, child care, nature camp, summer camp, theater, guest speakers, workshops and seminars, ESL classes and immigration documentation assistance, recreation, sports teams, holiday events, healing services. If your congregation offers and publicizes these events, people will learn about you in positive ways. If possible,

make meeting and office space available to the larger community and community groups.

- *Have a bring-a-friend Sunday.* Around 74 percent of all people who visit a church for the first time come because a member of that church told them about it or invited them.

TWENTY WAYS TO STEP OUT INTO YOUR CITY OR TOWN

1. March and / or carry a banner in parades and staff booths for pride parades, marches, etc.
2. Offer to do a library exhibition on the Transcendentalists, the Suffragists, or another topic.
3. Do a neighborhood walk. Who are your neighbors? Introduce yourself. Talk to them about their wants and needs.
4. Co-sponsor community events.
5. Have a van with your congregation's name on it.
6. List your congregation in the yellow pages.
7. Put up a Wayside Community Pulpit. (Order one from the Unitarian Universalist Association Bookstore.)
8. Have a gorgeous garden in front of your building and a community vegetable garden.
9. Plant trees. Plant a peace pole (a totem or maypole that displays symbols of peace).
10. Adopt a highway, river, beach, or trail.
11. Donate books to the library with Unitarian Universalist bookplates in them.
12. Put congregational bookmarks in the books you sell.
13. Have an interfaith holiday celebration or choir.
14. Sing holiday carols at the mall or downtown.
15. Have members sit on community boards of directors; let them know where they come from.
16. Have a refreshment or other booth at the county fair.
17. Have one "big name" program a year (an event that features a famous person) and donate proceeds to a particular cause or group.
18. Serve food to the homeless on a regular basis.

19. Serve coffee at a highway rest stop.
20. Try telemarketing (by yourselves or with other local congregations) or using the public access TV channel to air Unitarian Universalist tapes suitable for broadcasting (ask the Unitarian Universalist Association in Boston for recommendations, or write to the All Souls Unitarian Church of Tulsa, who produced a good one).

TWENTY WAYS TO STEP INTO THE LARGER UNITARIAN UNIVERSALIST WORLD

1. Regularly update your mailing list with the Unitarian Universalist Assocation so new members get the *World* magazine as soon as possible.
2. Have a quarterly discussion group that reads and discusses articles from the *World* and other Unitarian Universalist publications.
3. Start congregational email and develop a home page—your District Office wants to put you on the Web. Check out Unitarian Universalist chat rooms on the Web.
4. Develop joint programming with nearby Unitarian Universalist congregations. Share resources, skills, and cooperative training.
5. Ask your district staff to conduct board training for four or more boards at the same time.
6. Send delegates to annual district meetings. Sell soup and sandwiches after church to raise funds for the congregation to send delegates. Or dedicate a portion of unrestricted endowment fund interests to subsidize travel expenses.
7. Send delegates to the General Assembly.
8. Send congregational members to district and Unitarian Universalist Association training opportunities. Choose from Leadership School seminars, summer camps and institutes, conferences and mini-university training, and so on.
9. Join the Partner Church program and meet our Transylvanian brothers and sisters.
10. Sell books, Unitarian Universalist jewelry, bumper stickers, T-shirts, and coffee mugs in a congregational store.

11. Ask your minister to organize two or three ministerial pulpit exchanges with Unitarian Universalists and with other religious groups.

12. Invite a congregation of another religion you want to learn about to be partner churches. Have dinners for eight with four people from each group twice a year. Have a picnic or softball game together each spring.

13. Have a publications audit. Create a Publications Task Force to collect and review all congregational materials. Do you like your logo? If not, create a new one and a new look for all congregational publications, including religious education and committees.

14. With other local congregations, buy time on National Public Radio: Be one of the underwriters of your local station's programs.

15. Staff a PBS pledge drive, wearing congregational or Unitarian Universalist T-shirts.

16. Have a congregational Sunday workshop, perhaps combined with the service, to figure out what you say after you say that you are a Unitarian Universalist.

17. Order the wallet-card sized copies of the UUA Principles and Purpose from the UUA Bookstore. Or print the UUA Principles and Purposes on bookmarks with your congregation's name, address, phone, and Web address on them.

18. Visit other Unitarian Universalist congregations in the area. See how they do things to get ideas. Have your youth group meet with theirs.

19. Visit other denominations' congregations or synagogues in the area. Arrange for a religious education exchange with them. Have your youth group meet with theirs.

20. Do at least one smashing, complete, and real service for your city or town each year. Then get the word out to the media that you did it.

IS A SHOE HORN NECESSARY?

Public relations can be expensive and time consuming, but it doesn't have to be. Here are ideas for getting the results you want at the pace and price you can afford.

- *Fundraising and development:* Be sure to have a line item in your congregational budget for advertising, publications, etc. Your District Chalice Lighter program, the Unitarian Universalist Funding Panel, and other funding sources may be good possibilities to explore for special projects—contact your District Office or the Unitarian Universalist Association for information. Try attention-getting fundraisers like a well-known speaker or a monthly cabaret or coffeehouse. These can bring in money and focus public attention on your church as well. Sell congregational mugs and T-shirts—they are fun to use, catch the eye, and spread the word.
- *Publications:* Newsletters and brochures tell what we stand for. Using your creative brief, develop brochures to describe the congregation, its lifelong learning activities, and its path to membership. Make sure your minister, board, and staff have business cards. Print up pew cards for newcomers and congregational bookmarks to place in library books or books sold in the church bookstore. Order Unitarian Universalist Association and district brochures to inform guests about the larger movement.
- *Advertising:* Don't buy news, make news. Send out regular press releases about news on church events and members. Have a logo. Put it on everything. Put your mission statement on everything. Educate members to tell people they belong to your congregation. Get sample ads from the Unitarian Universalist Association. All program areas need to be attentive to newsworthy stories and events in advance to get media coverage. Send regular submissions to the religion page of your local newspaper. Put flyers up on bulletin boards and kiosks in libraries, laundromats, coffeehouses, and college campuses.
- *Merchandising:* T-shirts, buttons, bumper stickers, mugs, Unitarian Universalist bookmarks in gift books, Unitarian Universalist kazoos, personal checks decorated with chalices, ornaments, jewelry, pottery, bumper stickers, and return address stickers are all prospects for fundraising and publicity in the community.

EVANGELISM: YOU HAVE TO CRAWL BEFORE WALKING

Be comfortable talking about your congregation and what you love about it. This is the best way to evangelize Unitarian Universalism. If you don't know it, you won't believe in it. If you don't believe in it, you cannot convincingly tell others about it. To help you understand your congregation, do the Who Are We as a Congregation? exercise at a workshop or a coffee hour. Join up in pairs and do role plays. Remember to relate the Unitarian Universalist Association Principles and Purposes at work or in other places. If you are on a board or committee in community organizations, tell people that you are a Unitarian Universalist. If they ask about it, be prepared to give a concise, informative answer.

Another way to evangelize Unitarian Universalism is to teach children how to articulate our faith, beliefs, and principles. Once they become comfortable with their understanding of Unitarian Universalism, they will be better able to share our beliefs and traditions as they grow older.

MORE GOOD STUFF TO READ

Dunkin, Steve. *Church Advertising, A Practical Guide.* Nashville TN: Abingdon Press, 1990. A beginner's guide to sound advertising theory.

Webb, John David. *How to Change the Image of Your Church.* Nashville, TN: Abingdon Press, 1993. Communication as a fundamental for growth—how to develop literature, use technology, and discover the symbols and stories that help create a congregation.

CHAPTER SEVEN

Hands

Tell me a story.
Tell me what you are thinking about.
This congregation should care about social action.
Like?
Living the Unitarian Universalist story. Connecting our actions to our principles and history. Because social action is consistent with our heritage.
We need to find out what there is to do, and then—
Yes! Great! Let's do it! How can we help?
Let's find out. Let's get started! Let's call a meeting!
Yes! Let's do it!

Chapter 6, "Feet: Public Relations and Evangelism," was about discovering who we are as a congregation, stepping out into the world, and getting the word out to the larger community. One of the things we can tell the world is how well we care. Chapter 7 suggests ways to reach out through social justice, social action, and social concerns. This chapter asks us which good works we might do. Remember, our hands are connected to the rest of the body. They feel, they touch, they inform, and they do.

Ideally, every congregation will reach out to help and care about other people. The good work we do bears witness to our faith and our Principles and Purposes. Through reaching out and helping other people, we act on these. With our hands we welcome, testify, accomplish.

A community that only looks inward serves itself. It rarely commits to working on behalf of others. If we want to change the world, we must first change ourselves. Good works don't happen in a vacuum—they are accomplished by people who are connected to the larger world. To understand and emphasize that social action and spiritual growth go hand-in-hand is to become engaged in a larger purpose.

REACHING OUT: AN EXERCISE FOR EVERYONE

"And they shall repair the ruined cities and restore what has long lain desolate."

—ISAIAH

Not reaching out to others is about prejudgment. One Sunday morning, ask everyone in the congregation to look at the people around them. Ask them to silently identify one person they don't know or don't know well. Then have them silently ask themselves (or jot down): What is the age of that person? What is their level of education—high school, college, graduate degree, doctorate degree, or other? What is their line of work? Favorite foods? Politics? Are they introverted or extroverted? Intuitive or rational thinkers? Liberal or conservative? What kind of car do they drive? What part of town do they live in?

Now challenge the congregation by saying: "After the service, find that person and see how accurate your judgment is. The truth of the matter is that we make these kinds of judgments and assumptions about people all the time and everyday. We are wrong more often than we are right. Imagine the margin of error if that person is of another race, another gender, Jewish, gay, Catholic, Mormon, old, young, differently abled, or covered with grease!"

What might you assume about the people in this drawing? Write another caption for it.

Whenever we make prejudgments or errors in perception, we contribute to the power of evil. The most effective way to change these almost automatic misjudgments is to *unlearn* our racism, sexism, homophobia, all the "isms" that come between us and the realities of the world. Each person must find out who those "other" people are.

To know "others," to identify with them even in a small way is to begin to combat that which oppresses and deprives. And as we learn about ourselves, we begin to reach out.

Social justice is the partnership of people and need. Any congregation, by entering the rewarding, difficult world of social justice, social action, and social concerns, will be satisfied when it chooses and commits itself to the work. To identify the work, begin close to home. This entails understanding your community and its needs.

"Social justice is finding out what belongs to whom and then giving it back."

EXPLORING YOUR COMMUNITY

Put together a task force of people from your congregation to do research alone or in pairs. Identify the boundaries and qualities of your community by examining these simple questions:

- What are the physical boundaries? What is the geographic area in which the congregation is situated?
- What are the anchor institutions of the community: industry, schools, government, financial institutions, arts, major employers that define the community.
- What are community gathering places? Coffeehouses, malls, schools, libraries, parks, etc.
- What needs exist in the community? Who responds to them? Which ones match the skills, interest, and talents that the congregation has to offer?
- What are the hot community issues? Interview community leaders and ask them, "What are the issues of this community from your view?" Be sure to hear the stories of people not like you.
- Report to the Task Force on the information you gather. Discuss it. What questions arise? What additional information do you need to identify the right project for your congregation?

Meanwhile, begin to raise awareness of social justice needs in your congregation. Try one of the congregational exercises that follow on a Social Justice Sunday.

THE SOCIAL JUSTICE TIMELINE

This exercise helps members of your congregation identify what the congregation has already been involved in and to feel proud about it.

Before starting, hang the butcher paper on the wall. About half a foot below the top of the paper, draw a line in black, parallel to the top of the paper. At one end, put the date of the founding of the congregation. At the other, put the current date. Divide the space in between (by marking the decades above the line) into all the decades or years between the earliest date and the present date.

Introduce the exercise to the group: "Today we are going to identify this congregation's history of involvement with issues of justice. Let's start at the earliest date. I invite you to call out events, projects, history of our service and witness. Let's begin with our earliest accomplishments and move, decade by decade, toward the present."

Let members of the congregation call out events like: "In the 1960s we marched for civil rights." Or "We started a women's group in 1972." Or "We planted trees after the mountain burn of 1987." Or "We fed the homeless during the winter of 1994."

At the end of the exercise, say, "This roll call of our involvement will be up here for the next three Sundays. If you think of work we have done that is not here, feel free to add it on. And now let's have a moment of silence to remember what we have done and why we did it." (*Allow one minute.*)

Read "To Be of Use," Reading #567 in *Singing the Living Tradition.*

Close by saying, "And now, let's close with a rousing amen to celebrate our accomplishments."

PHILOSOPHY-MAKING EXERCISE

Hang butcher paper on the wall. Ask the group to brainstorm general areas of social justice, action, or concern in which they might want to be involved (world hunger, pollution, gay rights, peace, etc.). Write these ideas on the butcher paper.

Give each person three adhesive dots. Ask them to vote by placing their

One hour

Butcher paper, 10' or 12' x 4'

Masking tape

Water-based marking pens

Reading #567 from *Singing the Living Tradition*

One hour

dots on their top three choices. Write each of the three top vote-getters on a separate piece of paper.

Ask people to sign up on the paper that interests them most. The task of each group of volunteers will be to research their area, why it is important, what its needs are, and what moves them about these needs.

Ask each group to be prepared to present at a Sunday service the issues, feelings, programs, and challenges involved if the congregation were to take on work in the area. Be sure the music, the readings, and the sermon (given by the minister or someone else the group identifies) relate to the topic.

A FIELD STUDY WORKSHOP

This is an exciting and fun way to find out more about your town. Get a planning team together—the social concerns, justice, or action committee is a good possibility. Ask the minister and the board to be involved in and to support the planning. Set aside one Saturday from 9 A.M. to 5 P.M. for the workshop. Follow with a potluck (see instructions below) to celebrate the work. Plan for the next morning to be a Social Justice Sunday on the importance of participation in social justice work. Place the report findings on the walls of the entry, sanctuary, and/or social hour, with a sign saying: This Is Our Town.

OUT IN THE FIELD

Invite the entire congregation to participate by sending them special letters or postcards, announcements from the pulpit, articles in the newsletter, and phone calls by the planning committee. The more people who participate, the more effective, useful, and fun the day will be. Have registration in advance. You will need to know how many participants to prepare for.

Divide preregistered participants into six small groups, striving for a blend of new and old members, those who know each other and don't, old and young, with and without children, etc. Try to put couples in different groups. Put the name of each person on the outside of a packet, with their group number marked on the envelope.

Each packet should contain a map of the city, divided into six sections with highlighter, and marked section one, two, three, etc. (This will be the group

Butcher paper

Marking pens

Masking tape

Adhesive dots

Writing paper

One day

Markers

Pens

Butcher paper

Writing paper

Masking tape

9" x 12" envelopes

Copies of your city's map for each person

Bell

Chalice or candle

number.) Try to make map divisions that make sense, are within natural boundaries, and with boundaries that people recognize and understand. Each packet should contain the list of field questions, paper to write on, a pen, and tips for interviewing.

Have someone prepare coffee, tea, and fruit for the arriving time.

Let people know that child care will be available; the children can join in the potluck that evening. Arrange for child care and people to manage the kitchen and to clean up afterwards.

For the potluck, arrange for tables to be set complete with flowers and candles while people are out in the field and for someone to do the clean-up after the potluck other than the group members. Food will be provided by the participants as part of their day's tasks. Include coffee, tea, and water for before and after field work.

Field Study Questions
Who lives there?
Where do they gather—coffeehouses, bookstores, laundromats, etc.?
What are the hot political issues?
Where is help needed and what kind of help?
What is the character of the different neighborhoods?
What churches serve them? Are the churches attractive, welcoming, well cared for?
What social justice or community work do those congregations do?
What services, such as parks, recreation, social services, welcoming services, are offered by your community? Is there a community center?
Are the schools well cared for and convenient?

Schedule

9–9:30 A.M.	Arriving
9:30–10:00 A.M.	Orientation
10:00 A.M.–3 P.M.	In the field
3:15–4:00 P.M.	Small group preparation
4:00–5:30 P.M.	Presentations
5:30–6:00 P.M.	Get dinner ready
6:00–7:00 P.M.	Dinner
7:00–7:30 P.M.	Closing

Arriving

Have a welcome table with packets for each person according to group, but do not hand the packets out until the Orientation. Offer people refreshments.

Orientation

Different members of the committee can take different roles during the day, or one person can be the day's facilitator. The leader calls people together with a bell and opens the workshop with a few words about community work and involvement, such as the following:

> I don't know what your destiny will be,
> but one thing I do know:
> the only ones among you who will be really happy
> are those who have sought and found
> how to serve.
> —Albert Schweitzer

> It takes so much to be a full human being that there are very few who have the enlightenment or the courage to pay the price.
> One has to abandon altogether the search for security and reach out to the risk of living with both arms.
> One has to embrace the world like a lover, and yet demand no easy return of love.
> One has to accept pain as a condition of existence. One has to court doubt and darkness as the cost of existence. One needs a will stubborn in conflict, but apt always to the total acceptance of living and dying.
> —Morris L. West, from *Shoes of the Fisherman*

Light the chalice or a candle, singing "Make Channels for the Streams of Love" (hymn #299 in *Singing the Living Tradition*). Close by saying, "Let us begin today, to live with both arms. Amen."

In the Field

Explain that the goal of today's workshop is to find out everything you possibly can about your community. Point out the list of field study questions in the packets and ask participants to brainstorm others. Add the list of brainstormed items to the list in their packets.

Small Group Preparation

Divide people into six small groups by asking them to check the section number on their packets. Their task is to find out everything they can about their area during the five hours they have and to bring a food contribution to the potluck dinner that is representative of their area—enough for the number of people in their group.

Encourage the groups to split into pairs at some point to better talk to people. The morning should be spent in general information gathering, the afternoon in interviewing people in the neighborhood or seeking specific information. Suggest they think of this exercise as a combination adventure, treasure hunt, and research project.

Wish participants good luck and good hunting. Remind them to be back and ready to offer their group presentation by 3 P.M. They can come back earlier to prepare their presentation or do their preparation in the field.

Presentations

Each group has 15 minutes to present its findings. Questions will happen informally at dinner, too. All the information they have gathered should be saved by the organizing team and be displayed to the congregation beginning at the next service and for the next month.

Dinner

Food brought in from the field should be dropped off at the kitchen to be set out, buffet style. Encourage people to share stories and information at each table. Organize the dinner tables so that one person from each group sits at a different table.

Closing

After dinner ask people to form a circle. Use the same readings and music that were used in the morning.

"Right knowledge entails right action."

—PLATO

THE MORNING AFTER: SOCIAL JUSTICE SUNDAY

Ask your minister or worship committee to organize the service, incorporating stories (two minutes, for one person from each group) of the Field Study Workshop into the service. Have one person from the organizing team tell the congregation that this information will help everyone identify what kind of work the congregation could do for and with the community. Tell them what the process in the time to follow will be. Have the music for the service be consistent with the program. Ask your minister or speaker to talk about social responsibility, social justice, and social concerns.

You may want to include this visualization exercise or one that you create in the service:

A Social Justice Visualization

This exercise should take about five minutes.

Facilitator: "Please get comfortable by putting your feet on the floor and relaxing. Close your eyes. Take three deep, slow breaths: one . . . two . . . three. . . . Imagine yourself coming home from a night out. You turn into your street. You see that your house is burning. You are given a shopping cart and are told that you can make only one quick trip in and you can take only what you can carry out. What do you take? Visualize your house. Identify things of value to start letting go of. What do you want? What will you absolutely need? Imagine going through your house picking up what is most important to you, putting these things in the cart. You bring them outside. This is now all you own. What will you do next? How will you survive? Where will you go? Who will help you? What kind of help will you need?

"Slowly, when you have answered these questions, return to this room."

Facilitator pauses, and when everyone has returned their attention, says: "The homeless and the poor are only one part of our community of need. Most of us have never even begun to imagine what it might be like to be in such a place. Let us begin to think about how we may reach out and help others. What can we do? What are we willing to do? What ways can we imagine to help?"

This kind of visualization can be done on many subjects. Ask for volunteers to develop a visualization for the congregation before introducing a possible project for congregational approval. People are often resistant until

they experience the problem. Getting people to feel the need is an important beginning. Motivating them to action is a great beginning.

WHAT MOTIVATES PEOPLE TO ENGAGE IN SOCIAL RESPONSIBILITY?

belonging   cognition   curiosity

learning about the new and different

altruism   good works   meaning

leaving a mark   having a meaningful mission

being known in the world   pride   shame

faith   compassion   hope

. . . and the greatest of these is love.

In addition, you become visible and known in the community because you care, because you have a conscience that reaches out into the world. Through helping hands, you say: We are people who care, who take risks, who make mistakes and support each other even when we fall down. We are a loving and a beloved community.

GETTING STARTED: CONNECTING AND BUILDING COMMONALITY

- Identify people with shared interests and work.
- Plan a gathering to bring people together, such as a work party, and then share ideas.
- Invite people who are invested in this idea. Tell them you want to have on your team. Do this with personal contact, the newsletter, postings, or pulpit announcements.
- Tell stories (see Chapter 2, "Breath and Spirit: Animating Congregational Life"). Storytelling is about the spiritual roots of commitment

to social justice. Tell personal stories that describe what led you to social action.

- Choose a small action that will be successful such as writing letters to policymakers about an issue, creating a Unitarian Universalist social actions picture gallery, donating books to the church library or local library, or having a garden party to beautify the building (see Chapter 12, "Skin, Hair, Teeth, and Nails: Better, More Attractive Buildings").
- Celebrate your successes, then identify bigger projects to work on. Congregational recognition of your efforts is important.
- Take pictures and enlarge them for the church gallery.
- Use integrative curriculum for Lifespan Religious Education, focusing on peace and social justice as a spiritual discipline.
- Organize a social justice film series with coffee and discussion afterwards.
- Teach children to serve—let them identify, plan, and do a service project for the congregation, then the town.
- Plan a workshop on fear of social action—what will we lose if we do it? What will we gain if we are involved in our community?
- Have people who have done work in social justice place their handprints as a form of physical signature on a Social Responsibility wall or make their footprints in a cement path on a Social Responsibility walk somewhere on the congregation's grounds.
- If you have potters in the congregation, ask them to help create tiles for a Social Responsibility wall or path. Invite the congregation to purchase these tiles to commemorate a special project.

"Infinite gratitude to all things past
Infinite service to all things present
Infinite responsibility to all things future."

—ZEN SAYING

HOW DO WE CHOOSE A PROJECT?

Many congregations have a hard time choosing from many deserving projects. It is good for every member to choose work to do in the larger world. Building a house for Habitat for Humanity or adopting a road or a river is fun and useful.

How does a congregation make this kind of choice? Here is a process created by the members and friends of First Parish in Framingham, Massachusetts, which other congregations have adapted successfully.

One to two hours for each meeting; scheduled for after the Sunday service.

Newsprint

Markers

Masking tape

Adhesive colored dots (three for each participant)

Publicize each meeting in the church newsletter and the order of service for the three preceding Sundays. Ask people to bring a brown bag lunch. Provide drinks and child care. Choose a facilitator for the process.

THE FRAMINGHAM PROCESS

This process takes place over a series of large and small group meetings. The Social Concerns Committee is a good group to present it, although a special interested group can be formed for this process.

First Meeting

The task of this first meeting is to brainstorm all possibilities for a congregational social justice project. Explain the process to the group and say that this meeting is the initial step. You might share projects that other congregations have accomplished: sanctuary housing for a Central American family; defeating a proposed incinerator initiative and starting a recycling center instead; defeating right-wing religious candidates for the local school board through a forum series open to the community; planting trees in the local forest; volunteering at a prison; and adopting a mile of river to clean up twice a year by canoe.

Explain that ideas for a social justice project should be something that can be accomplished in a year's time. Next year this same process will be used to identify another, new project. Outline the brainstorm ground rules (no discussion, everything goes on the sheet) and, using markers and newsprint, brainstorm the list. Try for at least 12 projects on the list that represent a spectrum of interests.

When the list is complete, distribute three sticky dots to each person (only church members vote) and ask them to place the dots by their top three choices, putting only one dot on a given choice.

Count up the dots and circle the top three choices. If there is a tie for third place, include both choices. Ask for volunteers to sign up for a task force for each choice. Ask them to agree on a date for their first meeting. Give each task force the following instructions:

- Find out everything you can about this project.
- What encourages us as a congregation to work on its behalf?
- What discourages us?
- How will we help? With time, money, people?
- What is a good timeline for the project?
- Why should this congregation get involved?

Give each task force three months to research its project, develop a plan to propose, and write it up. Each of the three plans should be distributed to every member of the congregation by mail. Forums or Q&A sessions can be held for people to learn more. A second congregational meeting should be held for discussion and voting on one of these three choices for the congregational service project. It is important that everyone understand and agree that only one choice will be made for each year.

Second Meeting

This meeting is also held after a Sunday service. Again, ask people to bring a brown bag lunch. Provide drinks and child care.

Ask each of the three groups to do a brief (ten-minute) presentation of their project. Leave 20 minutes for questions and discussion. Hand out ballots, take a vote, and count and announce the results. Send around sign-up sheets for the project after the announcement. The project should be announced in the newsletter with an enthusiastic article. Be sure to let people know that the process will be repeated annually and that each year, a new project will be proposed. Of course, you can choose the same project again.

SOCIAL JUSTICE WORSHIP AND CELEBRATION

It is hard to be a Unitarian Universalist without seeing the relationship of our principles to social action. We can articulate this relationship on Sunday mornings. Celebrate the good works of your congregation with topical Sunday mornings. Talk to your minister about how you can do this, or bring it up at a Worship Committee meeting.

TWENTY WAYS TO STRENGTHEN THE RELATIONSHIP BETWEEN UNITARIAN UNIVERSALIST PRINCIPLES AND SOCIAL RESPONSIBILITY

1. Use biblical references that encourage social responsibility in the Sunday service.
2. Have a one-minute history moment at every service, celebrating the accomplishments of famous Unitarian Univeralists, particularly activists.

3. Give three-minute Unitarian Universalist history lessons on living our principles and the people who did that.

4. Hold a prejudice reduction service. Invite people to take the pulpit and share their stories and their beliefs. (See Twenty Ways to Unlearn Racism in this chapter.)

5. Offer congregational leadership training. Send members of the congregation to district and Unitarian Universalist Association trainings in social justice.

6. Plan special celebrations and services on holidays, such as Martin Luther King, Jr. or Arbor Day; invite a guest speaker.

7. Have a congregational social action sing-along one morning.

8. Have a community-building service: Share the results of your Field Study Workshop in a service.

9. Hold a nurture and celebration service recognizing the social justice activities of the year and their activists. Choose a social justice volunteer of the month. Put his or her picture on the wall with a brief paragraph describing the work they did. Designate a special "Volunteer of the Month" parking space for them or devise some other reward.

10. Put together a Unitarian Universalist Service Committee Sunday. Ask your district UUSC representative for help with materials. Put membership flyers in the order of service. Participate in Promise the Children.

11. Make masks of different cultures (perhaps the high school youth would enjoy doing this) for display in the sanctuary. Perform a Greek or other play for the service using the masks.

12. Present a chancel drama on a Unitarian Universalist historical activist and create a dance theater group to do multicultural dances.

13. Start a street theater troupe to go out to a public park during the year and act out social concern topics.

14. Have the youth group make a video documenting congregational service projects. Schedule a "major studio feature preview" and reception for the participants and families. Sell popcorn and let the kids decide where the money goes.

15. Invite singers and musicians from different cultures for Sunday services on the holidays of other cultures.
16. Make a quilt and pass it around to members who are sick, birthing, or dying.
17. Make a multicultural quilt (each patch a different culture), raffle it off, and give the proceeds to your social justice project group.
18. Use readings and poetry from other cultures.
19. Collect used books at a Sunday service to go to the local library or clothes for an abused women's or homeless shelter.
20. Have a pancake breakfast before the service and give profits to the homeless shelter.

HOW DO WE CELEBRATE?

- Have an affirmation Sunday and affirm what all members of the congregation do on behalf of the larger community.
- Cover a wall with butcher paper for graffiti where members can write everything they did to help others this year.
- Have a Sunday where everyone comes to church dressed as a hero or role model from history, literature, or mythology who did social justice work.
- Come to a Sunday social action service in a favorite social action T-shirt.
- Have a "forgotten heritage Sunday"—what we're proud of in our religious tradition and what we want to celebrate, but don't often think about.
- Give a daisy to everyone who has done a social action effort for the congregation.
- Put up a photo display of members at work on social justice efforts.
- Write thank-you notes or postcards to people who work especially hard or are especially compassionate, thanking them for their work. Or give them a call. Or take them to lunch.
- Create that honor path or wall.

"Don't tell me what you believe, tell me what you are doing."
—ROBERT FULGHUM

TWENTY HANDS-ON PROJECTS FOR CONGREGATIONS

1. Start a congregational food bank or a box for people to bring canned, boxed, non-perishable food to contribute weekly to a food bank. Consider serving as a homeless shelter or soup kitchen if you have a building. If you don't, or your building is not suitable, volunteer to help at other programs.

2. Organize a summer day camp for kids and reserve ten percent of the places for kids who can't afford camp. Or establish a camp fund with a local camp for a lower-income child.

3. Organize a van to pick up people who need transportation for church, church engagements, and other activities such as voting.

4. Start an after-school study hall for kids with tutoring in reading, math, and English as a second language. Include kids from a nearby school.

5. Let the congregation witness for social change at government sites, parades, and demonstrations by marching, setting up tables, etc.

6. Rent or give space in your building to community organizations. Have a concert at your church to raise money for them.

7. Do prison volunteer work. Ask your minister to help you identify a project.

8. Participate in Habitat for Humanity by building a house.

9. Offer your congregation Unitarian Universalist Association programs such as the Welcoming Congregation, Jubilee World, and Unitarian Universalists for a Just Economic Community and Faith in Action. Become familiar with the Diversity Initiative.

10. Is your congregation accessible? Do you have signing, hearing assistance in pews, Braille hymnals, mentoring programs? Do you target groups in the community before they come—the hearing impaired, the homebound, those who need transportation? Can you open your doors to them and truly welcome them? Have an accessibility audit of your facilities, then make the needed changes.

11. Have a Chatauqua for the larger community on social justice subjects once a year. Provide music and invite several speakers on different subjects.

12. Develop mentor programs for middle-school and high-school

youth, pairing them with adult mentors in the congregation.

13. Build church community partnerships: ecumenical partnerships, cooperative efforts with like-minded organizations, multi-church efforts, community development projects like a recycling center, teen center, or an interfaith coalition. Join the Interfaith Alliance.

14. Help create a needed community organization, such as a parenting center or an after-school child-care program. Spin it off and let it be independent.

15. Have a multi-congregation and multi-ethnic social justice camp.

16. Start a community garden if you have the land. Give the food to homeless shelters. Or maintain a flower garden on a neglected city corner.

17. Offer prayer vigils and candlelight services when the community needs them.

18. See that your minister or LIU laity are on the boards of community organizations.

19. Join county or regional task forces for citizen involvement.

20. Provide non-partisan public forums for local candidates and issues, bringing in various points of view.

TWENTY WAYS TO UNLEARN RACISM

1. Have people sign up for small groups of eight. Meet one night a week for ten weeks, two hours per night. Use week one to get acquainted and understand the process. Use week ten for celebration, reflection, and closure. Weeks two through eight offer each person in each group the full attention of the group: 15 minutes for opening; one hour for the person to talk; 30 minutes for group comments and reflection; 15 minutes for closure. Each person in turn talks about the following: my ethnic heritage as far back as I know about it; assumptions that are made about my people; how and where I learned those assumptions; which assumptions made me feel ashamed; what I love about my heritage; what I wish could be changed.

2. Have people sign up for small groups of eight. Structure as above. The topic (rotating each week from person to person): When did I

"Social justice is God's holy work. It is the work God left undone."

—RABBI DAVID SAPPERSTEIN

first realize that there were people different than I? How did I learn that? At home? In school? From friends? When did I begin to question these learnings? What do I know or feel now?

3. Find out if a group in your community is composed of people from your ethnic group. Go to one of their meetings.

4. Get a monthly lunch group together to eat at restaurants offering food from a particular ethnic group. Talk to the chef or the owner about the food you ate and what it represents culturally.

5. Start a cooking and eating club that rotates its menus from culture to culture.

6. Start a theater party group: Go to plays presented by small theaters that represent the drama or dance of different ethnic groups.

7. Start a video group that meets once a month to view and talk about films from various cultures and countries.

8. Put on a poetry reading evening/coffeehouse at your congregation. Invite local poets from other ethnic groups to do the readings.

9. Bring speakers from other countries to talk about their culture and their customs.

10. See if a nearby congregation is interested in participating in a 4x4x4 alliance. (See Chapter 6, "Feet: Public Relations and Evangelism" for more information.)

11. Initiate a Jubilee World program in your congregation.

12. Start a book group that reads texts by African-American, Asian, Hispanic, and First Nations authors.

13. Go to a powwow.

14. Visit a different congregation, temple, or synagogue four times a year.

15. Go to a mariachi mass.

16. Volunteer to teach English as a second language.

17. Call the Faith in Action office at the Unitarian Universalist Association. Ask them (or your District Office) to send you the brochure on programs and services they offer.

18. If you have room in your building, sponsor a folk arts and crafts fair for your community and invite artists and crafts people from many ethnic groups.

19. Celebrate one holiday per season in your congregation and church school from different cultures.
20. Put up a map in the social room of your congregation. Invite everyone to put an adhesive dot on the place each of their grandparents came from. Have a celebration of who you are.

BUDGETING FOR SOCIAL JUSTICE

Different congregations budget for social justice in different ways. For example, a 6,000-member Presbyterian congregation in Minneapolis pledges one dollar to social justice for each dollar pledged to the operating budget. Some congregations have endowed funds, earmarked for social justice purposes. These funds have been endowed through the generosity of members, through planned gifts. Some congregations have a special social justice canvass, like a capital campaign, with a panel elected to distribute the results. Grants are available from the Unitarian Universalist Grants Panel. The University Unitarian Church of Seattle has four special social justice fundraising times each year, with a specific project identified each time. Dances, concerts, arts and crafts fairs, and book sales are good ways to raise special funds.

"The real purpose of religion is human liberation," said the Buddha.

MORE GOOD STUFF TO READ

Canada, Geoffrey. *Fist Stick Knife Gun.* Boston: Beacon Press, 1995. A personal account of what it is like to live in the midst of and to fight against violent crime.

Coontz, Stephanie. *The Way We Never Were.* New York: Basic Books, 1992. The jacket reads, "This myth-shattering examination of two centuries of American family life banishes misconceptions about the past . . . seeing our own family pains as part of a larger social predicament means that we can stop the cycle of guilt or blame and face the real issues constructively."

The Earthworks Group. *50 Simple Things You Can Do to Save the Earth.* Berkeley, CA: Earthworks Press, 1989. Practical and entertaining.

Keen, Sam. *Faces of the Enemy*. New York: Harper & Row, 1986. An extraordinary book that tells us how ordinary people transform other ordinary people not only into enemies, but into monsters. Comes with a study guide.

Kozol, Jonathan. *Savage Inequalities*. New York: Crown Publishers, 1991. A moving description of what is happening to children in our schools, from poor families in the inner cities to the less affluent suburbs.

MacEachern, Diane. *Save Our Planet*. New York: Dell, 1990. A longer list than *50 Simple Things to Save the Earth*, with great supporting information and an abundance of ideas.

Heart

CHAPTER EIGHT

Creating and Nurturing Ministry

A Buddhist story tells us that there was once a poor man, beaten down by life, empty of hope and ambition, lying in a foul gutter, and . . .

there was a *sangha,* a religious community, a teaching community, with great heart and an open spirit, and . . .

the community lifted up the poor man, and embraced him as one of their own, and . . .

the community patiently loved and patiently taught him until he became whole. This man joined the community in love and eventually became the finest teacher-priest, the finest *roshi,* that the community had ever known. Each word and deed of this story is within the talents and capacities of any religious community that is willing to love intentionally with an open heart and to teach with respect and compassion. Such a community, says Robert Greenleaf, author of *Servant Leadership,* ". . . lifts everyone involved to a nobler nature." This nature is the heart of ministry. The heart of a congregation is ministry—how the congregation ministers to one another and how it is ministered to.

WHAT DOES MINISTRY MEAN?

The word "minister" stems from the Latin *ministrare,* which means *to serve.* As members of a religious community, we are bound to one another in faith. We serve one another in our community and so all become ministers. The person we call to serve us is our minister among ministers and may be described as *primus inter pares*, or first among equals.

WHO ARE THE EQUALS IN MINISTRY?

- *The members of the congregation.* In particular the members who serve the well-being of the bodies and spirits of the members of the community, such as lay ministers, caring committees, and other support groups.
- *The board,* whom the congregation has elected and empowered to work on its behalf and in whom it places its trust.
- *The staff:* the religious educator, the sextons, the people in the office.
- The *minister or ministers* called to be with the community as *primus inter pares.*

All these ministers, whoever they are, are committed and strong.

Caring is a calling to which all must be called. Ministry is for the openhearted, the gentle, the merciful, the forgiving, those who will not be driven off, those who bear witness. It is not for the faint-hearted.

CHECKING THE HEARTBEAT OF YOUR CONGREGATION

Ministry is about being open hearted, having love that is redemptive and freely given; paying attention to and caring about each other; tribal elders and brand new babies and children coming of age; celebrating marriage and mourning people who die. It is about heroes and heroines, myths and stories, struggles, and watershed events. It is about carrying our history and witnessing our lives.

Imagine the rhythms of the heart. Imagine the heart as it sustains the work of the body, how it pulses, beats, does its work day and night, day after day, year after year. Imagine how when some part of the heart fails, it is a crisis. Think about heartache and heartfelt reasons and matters of the heart and habits of the heart. How might these apply to a congregation?

Here's a simple process for checking congregational health around ministry.

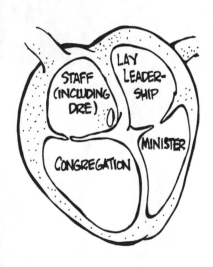

A HEART WORKUP

This would be a good check up for the Caring Committee or Lay-Ministry Group to do at their next meeting.

Brainstorm   (30 minutes)
On the butcher paper, have the group brainstorm the signs and symptoms of a healthy heart in a congregation.

Discussion   (45 minutes)
If more than ten people are present, divide into small groups. Distribute the following discussion questions to each group for discussion:

- Are we a welcoming congregation? How do we know this?
- How do we welcome and include new people? How do I?
- Do we have an active Caring Committee that keeps track of our congregational pulse? Do we have lay ministers? Do we have "beacons" (volunteers assigned to check-in with certain members who need help)? Do we have a telephone tree to get the word out when help is needed?
- Do we have a team of trained pastoral care people?
- Do we publicly recognize and thank people who volunteer? How often?
- What do the walls of our building say about the affection and respect we feel for one another?
- Do we have an archive to honor our history and elders?
- Do we have men's groups and women's groups? Support groups for caregivers? Job seekers? Or…?
- Do we have couples events? Events for singles? Families?
- Are we openhearted to our children? Do we have intergenerational services? Camps? Congregational events? Do we provide child care for all congregational events?
- Are our minister and staff fairly paid? Do we ever thank them for their work?

Three hours

Butcher paper

Masking tape

Several colors of marking pens

Copies of discussion questions for each person

Hang butcher paper on wall.

Comparison   (one hour)

Have the small groups check the signs and symptoms of your congregation against these questions. What does the workup tell you? Have groups report back to the large group and compare findings. Discuss.

Reassessing Congregational Habits   (30 minutes)

Consider doing or improving some of the things on the list of questions. Take a straw poll to see where you might reassess your congregational habits.

Form Task Forces

Choose just three things to accomplish this year as a congregation by listing ideas on butcher paper and having people vote for their top three choices. Recruit volunteer task forces to get things started. Write a motion for the Board to act on and an article for the congregational newsletter. Then go do the work. If we want to keep the heart healthy and strong we exercise. Consider the following aerobic heart exercises for a healthy congregation.

TWENTY TIPS ON BEING OPEN-HEARTED

1. Have each committee make a group portrait. Get a big roll of butcher paper, four feet or wider, and outline the members of the committee on it. Have members do their own self-portraits with crayons or colored pens. Have them write thoughts around their heads, where they have traveled by their feet, the food they like in their stomachs, and what they care most about over their hearts. Have each of them sign their portrait and hang the group portrait in the social hall or another place. Have a different committee do this exercise each month until all committees have done it. Include the board and the staff, too.

2. At home in a quiet moment, take your own heart inventory. Look at your calendar. How do you spend your time? How much in work? How much in play? How much time is used for matters of the heart, such as your congregation or work in the community? Discuss your inventory with others or at a circle supper one night. Ask others what they do to remain open-hearted.

3. The next time you see a rack of postcards, buy a dozen—or make some of your own postcards at home. Look through your congregational directory and address cards to people who have helped you, moved you, or been especially kind to others. Mail them, all at once or one at a time, to let others know you notice and care.

4. On some Sunday morning, have the congregation learn the Malvina Reynolds song, "Magic Penny." Give everyone a shiny new penny during the offertory—kids, too. Instruct them to give that penny away before they go home. Suggest they give it to someone they love, want to thank, or who needs a hug.

5. Talk to one person at coffee hour who is new or whom you don't recognize. Help them feel welcome by finding out where they are from and why they came. Find out what interests them and introduce them to someone in the congregation who can help them get involved with their interest. See if they have any questions you can answer.

6. Bend down. Talk to a kid for a few minutes. Be a friend.

7. If your congregation does not have volunteer recognition ceremonies, offer to help create one. (Give a daisy to everyone on a committee, a zinnia to committee chairs, and an iris to each board member, etc. Sing a joyful song from *Singing the Living Tradition*, like hymn #299, "Make Channels for the Streams of Love!" Have everyone hug each other or pat each other on the back. Have a volunteer fair afterwards so everyone can join an interest group if they haven't already.) Invent your own ritual—a wall of fame, a photo of the volunteer of the month, or a reserved parking space for the volunteer of the month. Announce the volunteer of the month in the newsletter, complete with a biography.

8. Honor your tribal elders. Have a special Sunday morning for them and suggest that the minister speak on a related subject. Choose three or four elders who have been around a long time and ask each of them to spend two or three minutes remembering how the congregation was when they first got there. Seat them in the front row. Give them a corsage or a boutonniere. Sing hymn #103, "For All the Saints," as they proceed out first into coffee hour. Have them form a receiving line.

9. On the anniversary of the congregation, have people bake cakes, one for each year or decade of the congregation's life to serve at coffee hour. Sing "Happy Birthday to Us."

10. Have a special evening to develop habits of the heart. Invite people in groups no larger than eight to each tell about a time when their heart opened up. What was it like? How long ago was it? Talk about what these stories have in common.

11. Find or take ten great photos of people in the congregation engaged in doing things together. Make sure there are faces and activity in the photo. Get them blown up to 2' x 3' or larger posters and hang them on the walls.

12. Bring the staff a box of homemade cookies or fudge.

13. Invite the youth—or someone—to create a video about the history of the congregation. Have them interview elders and former ministers and videotape old and new photographs. Schedule a major studio feature preview night with popcorn during the show and coffee and cookies afterwards.

14. Phone one person a month and tell them something you appreciated that they did and why.

15. Put spring flowers on the staff's desks and don't say who did it.

16. Send a bottle of fizzy cider, cheese and crackers, and a plate of fruit to the board the next time they meet, with a note that says, "Thank you for serving us so well."

17. Offer to serve on the Caring Committee or to organize a telephone tree if your congregation does not already have one.

18. Bring a casserole to someone who is bedridden or has a new baby.

19. Get a group together and make a baby quilt for a new baby.

20. Call on a convalescing or homebound member and bring some soup, flowers, or home-baked bread.

CARING COMMITTEES AND BEACONS

A Caring Committee is a group of volunteers who in smaller congregations contact each member every other month, in larger congregations, three times a year. They commit themselves to serve for two or three years, but often serve longer. They know people: who is sick, who had babies, who is worried or stretched. They let the minister know if someone needs to talk or suggest to the member that they might find it helpful to talk to the minister. They alert members of the congregation that Ms. X is bedridden and would like a visitor or some flowers; that the Ys just had a new baby and casseroles would help them; that Mr. Z has been worn out caring for his terminally ill wife and could use an afternoon off. They get the word out if there is important news to be shared. They mail cards of joy or concern on behalf of the congregation. They keep the minister alerted to the pulse of the congregation and the minister lets them know when there is work to be done.

Beacons are people assigned to a certain number of members of the congregation, usually not more than 10 or 12. They do the same things that Caring Committees do, but they are organized differently. Beacons are most effective when the congregation is spread out over a large territory or members live in many small communities rather than a more densely populated big one. Here is how people have handled matters of the heart in two different congregations.

- *The Wind Lake Unitarian Universalist Congregation:* John and Lila were beloved elders of the Wind Lake congregation. Lila was dying of cancer and wanted to die at home. John wanted to honor her wishes but did not know how to manage it—their financial resources were limited and care was expensive. The Caring Committee told the congregation what was happening. They asked who might be willing to volunteer one afternoon, morning, or evening a week, indefinitely. Open-hearted with love, members of this congregation went to John and Lila's house every day of the week, bringing food, cleaning house, reading to Lila, or sitting with her until the day she died peacefully, at home. They gave generously of their love and time and energy—yet most of them would say they received far more than they gave. This open-hearted congregation became stronger because of their love.

- *The South Ridge Congregation:* One summer there was a wildfire on one side of South Ridge. The Beacons called the members of the congregation who were closest to the fire. People from the congregation showed up with cars, vans, and trucks and helped the members near the fire evacuate. Members of the congregation housed the evacuees, helped them move into their homes when the fire was contained, and helped them clean up the damage. This congregation is an open-hearted religious community that cares for and about each other.

WHAT DO MINISTERS DO?

People often ask exactly what ministers *do*. We have many expectations of our ministers. Here's part of a funny list of what real ministers do, developed by Unitarian Universalist minister W. Edward Harris:

> Real ministers are never late.
> Real ministers don't ever use answering machines, voice mail, or email.
> Real ministers remember everybody's name.
> Real ministers stack the Board of Trustees.
> Real ministers have actually read every book in their libraries.
> Real ministers work only one hour a week.
> Real ministers are not afraid to take on the mother of the bride.
> Real ministers have children by immaculate conception.
> Real ministers' congregations are always growing.
> Real ministers always know who is sick and in the hospital.
> Real ministers don't go to coffee hour unless they want a cup of coffee.
> Real ministers are the last to leave the church.
> Real ministers know where the church vacuum cleaner is located.
> Real ministers don't need to print their sermons.
> Real ministers never worry about their sermons.
> Real ministers have perfect marriages.
> Real ministers make everybody happy.
> Real ministers never get involved in congregational arguments.

But what exactly do real ministers do with their time? In fact, most ministers work well over 50 hours a week and have many roles and responsibilities.

A copy of your minister's contract is probably on file in your congregational office. Look it over. If you really want to be educated about a day in the life of a minister, here is a light-hearted exercise that small groups in your congregation could try.

THE IN-BOX, OUT-BOX EXERCISE

This is a great exercise for a Committee on Ministry to facilitate with small groups of all members of the congregation.

Roles and Responsibilities
- It is raining. The sexton tells you as you enter the building that the basement is flooding.
- You have a call from Mr. Heavy Giver who is upset about the request from the Metropolitan Community Church to rent the building. Mr. Giver is afraid the children will be contaminated with AIDS. You know the Building and Grounds Committee has agreed to let the MCC use the building. You are sure Mr. Giver will want to take this matter to the board.
- Today is Friday and you haven't written your sermon.
- You have a memo from the chair of the Canvass Committee. He has decided it is not a good idea to canvass members individually. He wants to talk to you about it. The canvass starts next week.
- Your spouse left a message asking if you can pick up some groceries on the way home because some dear old out-of-town friends have just arrived for a surprise visit.
- You have a thick mailing from Unitarian Universalist Association headquarters with a lengthy survey to be filled out and mailed back before next Wednesday.
- The Religious Education Director comes in and tells you nervously that a crazy person has been wandering around the building asking for money. The person now seems to be asleep in a pew.
- You have a message that some members cleaning out the basement have come across a shoebox full of undeposited checks from 1978. The former treasurer, who has been dead for a decade, probably left them there.

90 minutes

Roles and Responsibilities Cards for each group

Index cards

Butcher paper

Marking pens

Masking tape

Photocopy the list of roles and responsibilities and cut them apart. Paste each role and responsibility on a separate index card. Make one set of cards for each group.

- There is an urgent message from a parishioner, Mrs. Whoopie D. Doo, who is somewhat of a hypochondriac, that she is desperately ill and needs to talk to you right away.
- You have an appointment to counsel a couple about their wedding in two hours.
- Ms. Friendly shows up at the door. "Hi! Just dropping by," she says, moving toward a chair to settle in for a chat.
- The secretary asks when you intend to proofread the newsletter.

Prioritizing

Distribute one set of Roles and Responsibilities Cards to each group. Say, "Imagine that you are the Reverend Allright. You come into your office bright and early one morning and here's what you face." (*Refer participants to the cards.*)

"You must read, assess, and prioritize each of these needs or demands on your time to begin your day. Each group has half an hour to arrange these cards by importance—from the highest, most immediate priority to the lowest, least immediate priority. Print them on the butcher paper. When you are done, we'll compare prioritized lists and discuss them."

Discussion

After everyone is finished, ask each group to present and post their list, one at a time, and explain how they made their choices.

Then invite people to comment and discuss. You might also have a copy of how your minister prioritized the list and why. Or you could invite the minister to be an observer and to comment after the group process is completed.

TYPES OF MINISTRY

Each congregation establishes the type of ministry, number of ministers, and titles of ministers within their community. Here are examples of the more common types.

LAY MINISTRY

Some congregations have lay ministers who may volunteer and then are selected and trained to assist the minister in pastoral duties. They may make hospital calls or calls on caregivers who are homebound. They are available in the minister's absence or when he or she is on sabbatical.

Lay ministers do not do pastoral counseling, but refer people to the minister or social services or agencies. They are familiar with their community's resources and helping professionals so they may refer people to what the larger community provides. Some congregations empower lay ministers to perform rites of passage such as weddings, memorial services, and child naming.

Training for lay ministry is always developed in consultation with, or by, the minister. Lay ministers meet regularly with the minister to keep him or her informed of the heartbeat of the congregation. For more information about lay ministry, call your District Executive.

PROFESSIONAL MINISTRY

Most congregations have one minister for whom they search, invite into candidacy, and call by a vote (usually 85 percent or more) of the congregational meeting. Mid-sized congregations may have more than one minister; large congregations almost always do. There are a number of different names or titles of ministers.

Settled Minister	Any minister in fellowship who has been called into settlement, by vote of the congregation.
Parish Minister	A minister who is called to and who serves a congregation.
Minister	Any ordained minister.
Fellowshipped Minister	Any minister who is in fellowship with the Unitarian Universalist Association—she or he has received credentials.
Senior Minister	Lead minister of a multiple ministry staff.
Co-minister	One of two ministers in peer relationship called to serve a congregation.

Community Minister	A minister who does not serve a congregation as its parish minister, who may be called or empowered in other work in the larger community. A chaplain, a community worker, or a minister serving an academic community are community ministers. Community ministers are engaged in special projects or organizations.
Minister of Religious Education	A minister whose training and special gifts call him or her to work in religious education, usually primarily with children and youth.
Assistant Minister	Serves a congregation in either a general or specialized capacity and is usually hired by the Senior Minister and/or a search committee.
Associate Minister	Serves the congregation in a general or special capacity, and is called to do so by vote of the congregation.
Interim Minister	Serves a congregation for one or two years while it searches for a called minister.
Ministerial Consultant	A part- (less than half-) time minister who usually serves small congregations that are considering ministry.
Intern Minister	A seminarian in a field-learning experience, supervised by the minister and an Intern Committee.
Extension Minister	A minister appointed by the Department of Congregational, District, and Extension (CDE) Services and affirmed by the congregation. An Extension Minister contracts for three to five years to serve a congregation that wishes to grow. The extension minister may be called as the settled minister of the congregation at the end of his or her contract.
New Congregation Minister	A minister appointed to the special task of ministry with a new congregation. Appointed

by the Department of Congregational, District, and Extension Services and may be called to serve the congregation.

THE CARE AND FEEDING OF MINISTERS

Most congregations are upfront and outspoken about what their minister does wrong. Not so many are outspoken about what their minister does right. Ministers like affirmation and compliments just like the rest of us.

Remember the Buddhist story about the derelict who became the finest minister of the community? Your congregation can be an openhearted teaching congregation, too. Here's a checklist for you to help with the care and feeding—and loving and teaching—of your minister.

___ Do you remember your minister's birthday?

___ Do you occasionally take your minister (and his or her spouse) out for dinner or invite them over?

___ When you have a concern or complaint, do you speak directly to the minister, and not about him or her to someone else?

___ Is your congregation committed to funding an outside facilitator if you want or need to have a difficult conversation? Or to calling the district for assistance?

___ Does your congregation support a sabbatical plan for your minister?

___ Does your congregation put aside $1,000 per year for sabbatical support?

___ Do people in your congregation give the minister kudos as well as critiques?

___ Does your congregation have a well-functioning Committee on Ministry (COM)?

___ Do people use the COM? Does the COM inform the congregation?

___ Can your minister be away without anxiety about what will happen? Is the rest of your congregational heart pumping well?

___ Does your minister need to be involved in every service?

___ Does your congregation have fair compensation awareness? Does it plan for raises and offer benefits?

___ Does your congregation support a continuing education plan for your minister?

___ Does your minister, with the board, have an annual plan of work with two or three top priorities for both minister and board? Did everyone participate in the plan and agree on it?

___ Is your congregation sensitive to, kind to, and embracing of the minister and his or her family?

___ Does your minister have the time and opportunity to listen regularly to members of the congregation?

___ Do you celebrate the important anniversaries in your minister's life, as well as the date when he or she was called to your congregation?

Each healthy congregation should develop its own creative habits of the heart in caring for and affirming its minister.

THE COMMITTEE ON MINISTRY

Committees on Ministry (COM) are designed to track the heartbeat of ministry within a congregation: how the members of a congregation take care of themselves and each other; how the lay ministerial leadership serves a congregation; and how the called minister serves the congregation. A healthy Committee on Ministry knows how well the whole body is being served by the heart. It seeks to understand, assess, support, and advocate for robust ministry throughout the context of congregational life. The COM makes recommendations about ministry in its many interactive dimensions.

The Committee on Ministry serves as a support group for the called minister, listening with respect, compassion, and confidentiality. It provides a channel of information and communication to and from the heart to all areas of the congregational body, moving back and forth to sustain, help, and invigorate the compassionate life of the congregation. In small congregations, the COM usually has three members; in larger congregations, five or six.

Some people feel that a COM should not take on the functions of a Ministerial Relations Committee (MRC) and so divide those functions. A Committee on Ministry serves the whole congregational body. A Ministerial Relations Committee serves the called minister. In such cases, it is good to have an MRC representative sit on the COM. Ministerial Relations Committees exist for the support and advocacy of the called minister only and do not assess, nor are

"Ministry can be like riding in a cattle car in the dead of winter—you appreciate the warmth of those around you; but you never know when you'll be stepped on, or worse."

—SOURCE UNKNOWN

they responsible to, the ministry of the entire congregation. A congregation should decide how it wishes to approach ministry—particularly or contextually.

CREATING A COMMITTEE ON MINISTRY OR MINISTERIAL RELATIONS COMMITTEE

There are several ways to form and structure a Committee on Ministry. The minister and board should discuss these ways and decide which is best for the congregation. The minister can appoint his or her own committee. The board can appoint the committee. Or both minister and board can appoint the committee.

- The minister can submit three names for each place on the committee and the board chooses one name from each three. Thus, if the committee is to be composed of three members, the minister submits nine names (for the first committee) and the board chooses three from that list. The three who are appointed serve three-year terms, so the first committee will have to determine who starts with a one-year, a two-year, and a three-year term, etc. Each year, one of the three members changes.
- The opposite can also work: The board submits nine names to the minister, who chooses three.

Generally, it is more supportive to let the minister submit the longer list—that way she or he is assured of having people on the committee who are comfortable to work with.

The longer list, however it is developed, should represent the diverse constituencies of the congregation: age, theology or philosophy, gender, parents or singles, etc. They should be people the congregation respects.

THE CHARGE OF THE COMMITTEE ON MINISTRY

Congregations vary, but board and minister should agree on the charge. The Unitarian Universalist Ministers Association *Guidelines* have specific suggestions for a Committee on Ministry, as does the Unitarian Universalist Association *Congregational Handbook.* The charge of the committee can be particular or contextual. For instance, a ministerial relations charge would be solely to support and advocate for the called minister of the congregation. A Committee on Ministry charge would be to support, inform, advocate for, and evaluate the ministry of the congregation in its entire context—including the called minister. It is a wholehearted approach.

EVALUATING MINISTRY AND MINISTER

Just as a good check-up is thorough and complete, so is a good evaluation of ministry. When your congregation begins its evaluation process, it is prudent to evaluate *contextually*. This means that every aspect of the ministry of the congregation is evaluated: clergy, staff, lay ministry, congregation. Be sure that everyone is familiar with the goals and priorities that have been established that year for minister, board, and committees of the congregation. The UUA Department of Ministry is currently developing evaluation tools that can help.

Evaluations should always be accomplished in relation to pre-established work goals and priorities. A person cannot be evaluated fairly if he or she does not know the criteria of evaluation. It is important to ensure that the evaluation process is thorough, fair, respectful, and compassionate. Here are four ways to approach evaluations:

1. a congregational survey
2. interviews and focus groups
3. ministerial self-evaluation
4. a combination of the above.

The following are four examples of evaluation formats. You may wish, with the minister, the Committee on Ministry, and the board, to consider which format you prefer or to develop your own process.

EVALUATION QUESTIONNAIRE

Adapted from an evaluation questionnaire by the Unitarian Universalist Church in Pittsfield, Massachusetts. This questionnaire was mailed to all voting members and the answers were collated by a task force.

Ministerial/Congregational Evaluation

This simple evaluation form provides an evaluation of the minister and a general evaluation of the way in which the congregation is fulfilling its purposes. It also provides for a self-evaluation of your efforts on behalf of this congregation. Score each evaluative item according to the following:

A = approve
D = disapprove
N = no opinion.

Please give the questions below prompt and thoughtful consideration. Please add written comments, either positive or negative, for these represent the most important part of this evaluation. Use the spaces provided, the back sides of this questionnaire, or attach additional sheets.

1. How is the congregation doing with respect to the following?

       Providing Sunday services to meet a range of needs.   ____
       Publicizing Unitarian Universalism.   ____
       Providing for fun and fellowship.   ____
       Providing religious education for children.   ____
       Addressing social concerns.   ____
       Offering adult programs.   ____
       Attracting new members.   ____
       Building a caring community.   ____
       Additional _____   ____
       Additional _____   ____

       Comments:

2. How are you fulfilling your role as a member of the congregation?

       Attending Sunday services.   ____
       Bringing my children to religious education.   ____

Serving on committees or other responsibilities.   ____

Participating in church-sponsored activities.   ____

Participating in democratic decision making.   ____

Making and paying my pledge.   ____

Inviting guests to services or other activities.   ____

Welcoming newcomers.   ____

Offering constructive criticism and also praise.   ____

Respecting others' views.   ____

Being sensitive to others' needs.   ____

Additional _____   ____

Additional _____   ____

Comments?

3. How is (name of minister) fulfilling (his/her) role as our minister?

Conduct of Sunday services.   ____

Quality of sermons.   ____

Counseling.   ____

Being available for counseling.   ____

Providing inspirational leadership.   ____

Being sensitive to people and their needs.   ____

Attending social functions.   ____

Furthering community and mutual caring.   ____

Providing support and resource help to religious education.   ____

Ministering to children.   ____

Planning and leading programs of personal
and spiritual growth.   ____

Working with the board and other committees.   ____

Performing weddings, memorials, dedications.   ____

Visiting the hospitalized and homebound.   ____

Keeping in touch with individual members.   ____

Involvement in interfaith activities.   ____

Involvement in the community.   ____

Participating in denominational affairs.   ____

Promoting congregational awareness and
involvement in the wider Unitarian Universalist movement.   ____

Demonstrating personal and professional growth.   ____

Additional _____   ____

Additional _____   ____

Comments:

4. What is your evaluation of this questionnaire? Please comment:

We ask that you sign this form in order to help us get as complete a reply as possible and to ensure our ability to respond to the concerns of particular individuals. Confidentiality will be maintained and the identity of respondents will not be shared with the minister without permission from the respondent.

_____

(signature)

So that prompt attention can be given to your opinions, praise, and concerns, please return your completed questionnaire by (date) and mail to: (name and address).

(You may wish to asterisk the primary working goals of the minister as identified by the minister and the board and include the following footnote: "* = established as a priority working goal. Please cross out any item which you consider irrelevant or unnecessary.")

STAFF INTERVIEW

The Committee on Ministry assigns each committee member the task of interviewing one or more staff person(s). The questions should be agreed on in advance so that each interview contains the same categories of questions. Generally, the questions should be open-ended, few, and broad in nature. You will, of course, adapt and develop your own questions, but as a rule of thumb, each staff person interviewed about the ministerial context and effectiveness of the congregation should be asked the same questions. Remember, you are not evaluating the staff person: You are asking them to help you evaluate the ministry of the congregation. Sample questions include:

- How well do you feel the congregation is doing with respect to meeting its needs and accomplishing its goals? (Articulate the goals if the staff person is unfamiliar with them.) Which needs are not being well met? Which need more attention?
- How are you fulfilling your role as a staff member? What do you wish you had more help with? What do you feel are your greatest challenges? From where do you experience the greatest support?
- How is your relationship with other staff? With the minister(s)? What is already strong? What could be strengthened?
- What do you see as the three great strengths of this congregation? The three great weaknesses?
- Do you feel that members of this congregation truly care about one another? How do you know?

FOCUS GROUP PROCESS INTERVIEWS

To develop focus groups, the board, minister, and Committee on Ministry should identify the constituencies of the congregation, taking into account groups or areas such as:

- gender
- age
- theological or philosophical views
- areas of interest in congregational life such as music, social action, etc.
- marital status and whether people have children
- length of membership in the congregation
- history with Unitarian Universalism
- degree of involvement in congregational life.

Ideally, all these diversities should be represented in each focus group, which should be balanced. All the focus groups together should represent the diversity of the congregation.

Depending on the size of the congregation, plan for one focus group of ten people per hundred members. Small congregations might have only two focus groups. Members of the congregation should be personally invited to participate in their focus group on a specific night.

All focus groups should be facilitated by teams of two members of the Committee on Ministry, one of whom should record the proceedings on butcher paper on the wall, so that participants can be sure their comments are being heard correctly. Groups should be asked three or four simple questions like the following examples. The same questions should be asked of each group. It is important that facilitators not attempt to lead the discussion.

- What did this congregation accomplish best this year?
- What did the minister accomplish best? The religious education director? The staff? The board?
- What are the most important areas of growth, change, or development for the minister? For the religious education director? For the staff? The board?
- What are the most important areas of growth, change, or development for the congregation?

When the focus groups have all taken place, members of the Committee on Ministry should get together and combine the proceedings. Together they should draft an Evaluation of Congregational Ministry and share it first with the minister, who should be invited to add comments in writing. Then the committee should present a finished report to the board and finally to the congregation. When writing the report, it is important to think in terms of accomplishments and successes and areas for growth and change rather than good and bad or right and wrong. Offer praise and affirmation, as well as concerns. Think in terms of the future, in terms of areas for growth and change.

Remember, evaluations are written for the benefit of those being evaluated, both congregation and minister. If you want change to occur, you must first be heard. If you want to be heard, write the report so that you have the greatest possibilities for compassion, openness, and good communication.

SETTING GOALS AND PRIORITIES

In the larger context of congregational work, the Committee on Ministry with the minister can approach a work year and develop a process for setting goals and work priorities with the board. From this process, a self-evaluation process for ministers can be naturally developed.

Remember the In-Box, Out-Box Exercise earlier in this chapter? Setting goals and work priorities is not so different from that.

Start the process by referring to the minister's contract and outline the general roles and areas of ministerial responsibility.

Refer to the Leadership Covenant, if you have one, to develop this list. Refer to any work priorities developed with the board.

Have the minister keep a log of work activities for a month, including office time, pastoral calls, sermon preparation, counseling, social action, and so on.

With the Committee on Ministry, categorize the tasks and work listed above in relation to these categories of ministry:

- teaching
- preaching
- administration
- church financing and finances
- congregational relationships
- growth
- pastoral work/counseling
- community outreach
- social justice/prophetic ministry
- denominational relationships (district, Unitarian Universalist Association, Unitarian Universalist Ministers Association, Liberal Religious Education Directors Association)
- personal growth and education
- balance of personal and family life with work.

Identify what is most satisfying and most frustrating. Prioritize the above, as with the In-Box, Out-Box Exercise in terms of importance for the year ahead.

With the Committee on Ministry, review and discuss what has been done. Consider what, in the context of the congregation's and the board's work, has the highest priority for the coming year. Identify two or three major priorities. Discuss these with the board and ask for their affirmation of the work goals. Plan to review progress periodically at COM meetings.

This process may be reviewed and/or repeated annually, and can become a foundation for ministerial evaluation.

By understanding the rhythms of your congregational heart, you learn to accept the fact that different people, different committees, and different tasks have different cycles. Ask yourself: When do we elect, train, honor, and celebrate our ministerial tasks, our habits of the heart? How can we develop great habits of the heart?

MORE GOOD STUFF TO READ

Beard, Margaret L. and Roger W. Comstock, eds. *All Are Chosen: Stories of Lay Ministry and Leadership.* Boston: Skinner House Books, 1998. A collection of personal, in-depth narratives about the work of shared ministry.

Hoertdoerfer, Patricia and William Sinkford, eds. *Creating Safe Congregations: Toward an Ethic of Right Relations.* Boston: Unitarian Universalist Association, 1997. A workbook of a collection of essays on a variety of congregational topics accompanied by discussion guides.

Hudson, Jill M. *Evaluating Ministry.* Bethesda, MD: Alban Institute, 1992. Principles and processes for clergy and congregations—exploring a new approach to evaluation as a total appraisal of congregational ministry, not just the pastor's ministry.

Unitarian Universalist Association. *Guidelines for Unitarian Universalist Ministers.* Boston: Unitarian Universalist Association, 1998. Ministerial code of practice and ethical guidelines. Available from the UUA Department of Ministry.

UUA Review and Renewal of Ministry Working Group. *A Guide to Review and Renewal of Ministry in Unitarian Universalist Congregations.* Boston: UUA, 1998.

"We are what we repeatedly do. Excellence, then, is not an act, but a habit."

—ARISTOTLE

Drafted June 1998 by the Review and Renewal of Ministry Working Group. Available through the UUA Department of Ministry, (617) 742-2100, ext. 437. Price $10.

White, Edward A. *Saying Goodbye*. Bethesda, MD: Alban Institue, 1990. About leaving, whether it is a change of vocation, retirement, conflict, or death.

Liver

CHAPTER NINE

Dealing with Congregational Conflict

In the human body, a healthy liver processes junk that we are not aware of. Healthy congregations process junk, too, by dealing with conflict appropriately. When the liver gets blocked up, the body becomes uncomfortable. When congregations get overloaded with unresolved conflicts, they become stressed and bad things happen. Worst of all, a dysfunctional liver can lead to other types of failures within the body.

There are different levels of dysfunction or conflict. Generally, the lower the level of conflict, the more easily and quickly the conflict will be managed. The higher the level, the more difficult management becomes.

Some experts in conflict assert that it is never really possible to resolve highest level conflicts. They say that the healthiest path a congregation can take is that of prevention and management. Conflict, when openly addressed and well managed, can be a strengthening and transforming experience. Not all conflict is bad: The Chinese character for *crisis* is a combination of the characters for danger and opportunity.

LEVELS OF CONFLICT

Dr. Helen Bishop, District Administrator of the Central Midwest District of the Unitarian Universalist Association, describes five types of conflict, each with different symptoms and requiring a different solution. These are adapted from the levels of conflict theory developed by Speed Leas in his excellent book *Moving Your Church Through Conflict*. They are, in increasing order of seriousness:

1. *The Problem.* Emotions are not involved; we consider the issues rationally. No facilitator is needed.

    Symptoms: Differences and conflicting goals exist. Feelings of discomfort in each other's presence, short-lived anger, denial of hostile feelings.

2. *The Disagreement.* In addition to (1), issues are associated with personalities and people may stop sharing information.

    Symptoms: Objectives of conflicting parties tend toward self-protection. Elements of shrewdness and calculation. Language shifts from specific to general. Hostility, negative humor, and derision are present.

3. *The Contest.* Factions form and mudslinging begins. As faction-like group-think takes hold, information is distorted, and questioning a faction's "party line" can mean ostracism.

    Symptoms: Shift from self-protection to winning. Objectives become more complex, sometimes clustered into issues and causes. People begin to take sides, seeking victory. Overgeneralization, distortion, magnification. Personal attacks are common.

4. *The Crusade.* The factions not only want to win; they want the other side to leave. Each side sees itself as principled and the other side as immoral. Some members may quit. Congregations may seek to fire their ministers.

    Symptoms: Objectives change from winning to wanting to hurt and/or get rid of others. The good of the issue is more important than the good of the group. Being right and punishing become the themes. Factions solidify; leaders emerge; language becomes ideology; there are attempts to recruit sympathetic outsiders.

5. *The War of the Worlds.* Members not only want the minister fired, they want to make sure he or she never works as a minister again. They not only want the other side to stop; they want them to leave. Congregations may split over a level-five conflict and attorneys may be needed. Level 5 is usually too late for facilitators.

   Symptoms: Objectives here are to destroy others. Opposition is seen as harmful to the group and needs to be removed. Parties see themselves as fighters for the eternal cause. They can no longer choose to stop fighting.

THE SYMPTOMS OF A CONGREGATION IN CONFLICT

- low levels of conflict are not dealt with and go underground
- calls for petition to impeach board, ask for the minister's resignation, etc.
- rampant gossip
- closed groups and secret meetings
- whispering campaigns about a person or a group
- letter-writing campaigns
- email and telephone cliques
- triangulation (talking about the person(s), not to them)
- inferring rather than directly expressing concerns
- abrupt changes in support of and participation in church life
- turf wars
- ineffective Committee on Ministry
- high staff turnover
- resistance to change
- unexplained resignations or departure of members
- transitions are catalysts for other complaints

CAUSES OF CONFLICT

Here are some common causes of conflict. If you notice conflict in your congregation, scan the list and see if the cause is there or look at the causes and see if any of them create potential for conflict in your congregation.

- *Human nature.* Almost all people want to function well and want to be in relationship. When they are dysfunctional or feel excluded from relationships, people experience or generate conflict. Conflict also occurs for purely personal reasons: greed, jealousy, attachment, fear, control, neediness, or vengeance.
- *The reality of brokenness and denial.* There is craziness and there are unreasonable people in the world. Sometimes we have to let people know, in a caring way, what the boundaries of behavior are.
- *External stresses.* A congregation may experience income or membership decrease. In smaller congregations, leaders may feel burned out. Stress and conflict among individuals may be a response to these or other external causes.
- *Resistance to change.* Conflict occurs with resistance to change. People resist change for a variety of reasons, but when the purpose of change is unclear, the mystery or ambiguity can cause anxiety.
- *Fear of change* can be as disruptive as change itself, producing the same worry and unrest. When change is being promoted for personal reasons, rather than the good of the community, conflict is likely to occur.
- *Poor communication about change.* When congregational communications are ineffective, resistance may occur.
- *Fear of failure* often accompanies conflict. This feeling is especially strong when the principals have not been consulted in changes, such as the restructuring of duties or committee job descriptions, and feel their performance has been judged.
- People resist change if there is a *lack of respect and trust* in the people who are initiating the change. Lack of enthusiasm and objections will surface quickly and the potential for conflict increases.
- *Satisfaction with the status quo* can mean more resistance to change. People fiercely defend the *status quo* even when change is necessary.

But conflict and change are normal and can be healthy and transformative. It is not processing the conflict and change that creates problems, blockages, upset, or toxic behavior. There are two ways to process conflict in a congregation: first, within the congregation, or second, by "calling the doctor," seeking outside help.

HOW CONGREGATIONS CAN PROCESS AND PREVENT CONFLICT

A congregation that processes conflict regularly and effectively has essential healthy behaviors, such as:

- open communication
- no secrecy
- no gossip
- civility
- agreed-upon boundaries and accountabilities
- well-developed skills in active listening (see Chapter 4, "Fostering Good Communications")
- assured opportunities for everyone to be heard and the understanding that conflict can be healthy
- commitment to seeking skilled facilitation when necessary
- strong sense of self-esteem.

In addition, the essential structures of the congregation are working if these are present:

- a congregational covenant of good relations (see "Covenanting Against Conflict" later in this chapter)
- skilled facilitators within the congregation
- open, trusted, trained leadership
- an agreed-on conflict management policy
- a working Committee on Ministry
- personnel policies (see Chapter 1, "Brain: Core Documents for Your Congregation")
- an active Personnel or Staff Relations Committee
- representation of the diversity of the congregation in the leadership.

In a healthy congregation, the power is spread out and around and then the positive prevails. The power is spread out because:

- All members are always invited into the power structures.

- There is no tyranny of the minority.
- There are systems for handling destructive or poisonous people.
- Decision making is open and inclusive.
- Congregational meetings or focus groups encourage discussion.
- Power is used to accomplish the goals of the congregation.
- Members are given information with which to make decisions.
- Members willingly accept the responsibility to make decisions.

The positive prevails because:

- The congregation deals with its conflict and pain and moves on.
- The congregation encourages dialog and reconciliation; the congregation cares for the community as well as individual members.
- The congregation publicly celebrates the resolution of conflict.
- Conflict prevention training is offered regularly.
- The congregation knows how to listen actively.

PROCESSING ASSUMPTIONS: THE HAT EXERCISE

We make inferences and assumptions about people all the time. Making these assumptions can be hurtful, excluding, and conflict-producing. Here's a lively way to discover just how many assumptions we make and how easy it is to make them. You can try this exercise with your board of trustees or at a leadership retreat.

Who Am I? Descriptions

HARD WORKER—Rely on me.
EXPERT—Heed my advice.
TALKATIVE—Keep me quiet.
COMEDIAN—Laugh at me.
IGNORANT—Inform me.
INSIGNIFICANT—Ignore me.
IMPORTANT—Defer to me.
FLAKY—Tolerate me.

One hour

Masking tape

Marking pen

12 strips of blank paper,
6" x 30"

Write each of the Who Am I? descriptions on a separate strip of paper. Keep the strips in a pile, face down, so that no one can see them.

HELPLESS—Rescue me.
SLOW—Patronize me.
OBNOXIOUS—Argue with me.
QUIET—Draw me out.

Process

This is an exercise for 12 people; if you have more than 12 people, let the remaining people be observers. If you have fewer than 12, choose the strips you wish to use to suit the number.

Tell the group that each person will receive a "hat" with words on it. Instruct them not to reveal the words written on any other person's hat and ask them to remain silent until they have each received a hat.

Place one strip like a crown, fastened at the back with masking tape, on the head of each person. The lettering should face the front. Do not let the person wearing the hat see what it says.

When each person has a hat, give the following instructions: "Please sit in a circle. You are all members of the Board of Trustees of the East Cupcake Unitarian Universalist Congregation. You are at a board meeting. (*Assign one of them the role of president.*) You are discussing the agenda for the upcoming board retreat.

"Treat each person as their headband says. You have about ten minutes to role play the board meeting."

At the end of ten minutes, stop the role play. Ask if anyone has guessed what their hat says. How did they know? How did it feel to be treated that way? Continue around the circle until each person has guessed or described their category.

Ask the participants to imagine what it must be like to be boxed into a category so that people make assumptions about you. Then discuss the fact that we all do this to people, in one way or another, every day.

Ask for observations and what they have learned from the process. How can we begin to do things differently?

You may wish to follow this with the Active Listening Exercise described in Chapter 4, "Ears: Fostering Good Communication."

WORKING WITH PROBLEM PEOPLE IN MEETINGS

Sometimes we get angry, annoyed, hurt, or full of pity and we don't know why. When this happens, it's good to see if we understand the dynamics and what our contribution to the upset might be. The first thing to do is to try to understand what is happening with the other person and with ourselves. Here's a chart, developed by Don Dinkmeyer and Gary D. McKay in their book *Systematic Training for Effective Parenting,* that helps identify what might be going on in some cases and makes suggestions about how to proceed in meeting situations. This is a guide, not a panacea.

If you feel:	then the other person's goal may be:
annoyed	to get attention
angry	to control—this is a power struggle and chances are that the person feels put down or diminished
hurt	to get revenge—they have been hurt themselves
inadequate	to prove themselves helpless

Unless the conditions change, the other person may not stop their behavior. Here are some specific suggestions for working with problem people.

If a person is:	then try:
an "I can't-er" or an "I don't know how-er" or an "I tried it already-er"	not to argue with them. Ask them to tell you all the reasons why they can't. Then ask them, "But if you could, what would it be like?"
shy	calling them by name, saying: "Mary, I'm so glad you came," or "John, I'll see you next time." Mention them by name and/or ask for their help with a short-term task.

an overwhelm-er	asking them to sit next to you and if they start to overwhelm you, put your hand gently on their arm. Overwhelm-ers like to be asked to do specific things and to be acknowledged.
very negative	asking yourself if this is what the person wants to be doing. If many people in a group are negative, go around the circle asking each person to complete the sentence: "I'd rather be . . . "
apathetic or bored	finding out if they really want to be there. If they don't, talk about it first and be sure they feel they have permission to leave, resign from the group, or work on doing things differently.
boisterous	asking yourself if people have been sitting too long. Take a break. Try moving.

If a meeting is not going well, take the time to ask: "Is this group doing what it really wants to be doing? Am I trying to make them do what I want to do? Do they really know what is expected of them? What are my assumptions about these people and this meeting?" It is always best to acknowledge a problem, whether in an individual or a group. If it is a big problem, a conflict, then set aside the time to explore it together and decide how you will handle it.

COVENANTING AGAINST CONFLICT

Congregations can have thoughtful conversations about how they will relate to one another. They can ask their District Office to facilitate a conflict prevention or request a communications workshop for the whole congregation. The minister or an invited guest speaker can preach on the subject of conflict. Workshops like these are wonderful for personal development, too.

Some congregations have had thoughtful conversations and then made agreements. Here are two examples, the first used for a small group or a committee.

**The Worship Committee Process Covenant of the
Michael Servetus Unitarian Universalist Fellowship, Vancouver, WA**

We listen attentively
and allow others to finish expressing themselves,
interrupting only in a respectful and
straightforward manner.

We speak always with respect.
There is no place here for ridicule or intimidation.

We each speak for ourselves alone,
unless representing the views of specific others.

We actively encourage
the participation of all committee members
in our deliberations.

We attend to the integrity of our covenant,
when necessary interrupting discussion
to raise a process concern.

This is a responsibility we all share.

**The Congregational Covenant of Good Relations of the
Unitarian Church of Victoria, British Columbia**

We, the members of the Unitarian Church of Victoria, agree to treat ourselves
and each other fairly and respectfully. We are committed to improving the
quality of our lives by supporting self-development, spiritual growth and the
use of our skills and talents in fulfilling and responsible ways.

Guidelines
The congregation agrees that by accepting and practicing the following attitudes
and actions, we will begin to fulfill our covenant of good relations. We also

acknowledge that each of us has within ourselves additional ways to contribute to this ideal.

Self

I am an individual aspiring to be a fully integrated, responsible and actualized person within my family, at work, and within my community.

I believe that to be successful, I must take responsibility for my personal well-being and that I must value myself. By doing so, I will be better able to understand and serve others, my church, and the larger community.

I will make the kinds of choices that balance my various needs with the needs of others.

I will make a commitment to learn the necessary skills to communicate in clear and sensitive ways.

I will nurture my spiritual needs.

Member to Minister

I will treat the minister and the minister's family with dignity, respect, and consideration.

I will look for occasions to offer sincere praise.

I will respect the personal time of the minister and the minister's family.

I will support and encourage the minister to exercise a responsible freedom of the pulpit.

I am responsible for nurturing my own spiritual growth and acknowledge the ministry as an important resource for this development.

I take responsibility to address differences of view with the minister and to deal with them in a personal way first, before taking them directly to the minister.

I take responsibility to address unresolved issues between myself and the minister by seeking advice from the Committee on Ministry or by following the appropriate procedures as set forth in the Conflict Management Policy. (See the next section, "Internal Management of Congregational Conflict.")

As a member of the Unitarian Church of Victoria, I will respect the UUMA's Minister's Code of Professional Practice and will refrain from conduct that will be harmful to or endanger the integrity of the minister.

Member to Staff

I will be courteous and respectful in my interactions with staff.

I will make only reasonable requests and will work with staff to determine the best method to get the work done.

I will respect the staff's work hours and the personal time of staff and their families.

I will acknowledge, or offer sincere praise for, work done.

In situations where I have an unresolved difference of opinion with a staff member, I will seek an appropriate resolution with the assistance of the UCV Conflict Resolution Team and the Personnel Committee.

I will support reasonable and fair compensation for staff services.

Member to Board

My role does not stop when the board is elected.

I will actively support, encourage, and show my appreciation to the board by being responsible for providing feedback when it is sought and making my expectations clear to the people I have chosen to represent me.

I will participate in the life of the church by using my skills and talents through taking part in committee and volunteer work where, and when, it is possible to do so.

I will support the church financially to the best of my ability.

I accept responsibility to learn how the church operates and will seek information through the various channels such as neighborhood groups, committee chairs, board members, bulletins, and the order of service.

Member to Member

I believe that each person is free to make choices regarding their personal journey. I will respect these choices and will support the spiritual growth of others in an inclusive, loyal, and generous manner.

I aim to actively listen to what others have to say.

In clearly communicating my needs, sometimes I will have to decline or say "no."

I will also honor the rights of others to do the same.

I will not engage in harmful gossip. I will be responsible for getting the facts for myself.

I will respect absolutely the confidentiality and private disclosures of others.

I will not claim sole ownership of any role or task while still recognizing the need for accountability.

I will make every effort to be aware of my emotions and to be sensitive to the emotions of others, recognizing these signal meaningful issues requiring empathy and guidance. In this regard, I will learn the necessary skills if needed and undertake the appropriate actions to express my emotions and beliefs in a constructive way.

I will be respectful of the private and intimate bonds of other members and not exploit the needs of another person for my own.

I will make every effort to settle issues between myself and another member on a one-to-one basis. If this is unsuccessful or unsatisfactory and I feel the need for further action, I will forward my concerns to, and follow the recommendations of, the UCV Conflict Resolution Team.

I will welcome new members and guests and commit to getting to know people in this religious community.

I appreciate that I am a member of a religious community that makes decisions through a democratic process. As a responsible citizen in this community, I will actively participate in the process and will respect the outcomes of the collective wisdom.

Member to the Community at Large

I believe in the inherent worth and dignity of every human being and will try to live my life in a way that encourages equality and compassion in human relations.

I will act responsibly in local and global issues in order to promote a world community with peace, freedom, and justice for all.

I respect the interdependent web of all existence. I respect and uphold life, and will live in harmony with the rhythms of nature.

In Closing

This covenant aims to complement the following documents of the Unitarian Church of Victoria:

The Unitarian Universalist Statement of Principles and Purposes
The Unitarian Church of Victoria Mission Statement
The Unitarian Church of Victoria Constitution and Bylaws
The Unitarian Church of Victoria Conflict Resolution Policy
The Unitarian Church of Victoria Sexual Misconduct Policy

Now ask yourselves: What are the process agreements in the committees of our congregation? What guidelines, covenant, or code of conduct informs the good relations and behaviors of our congregation?

Such processes should involve, as in the first example, the whole committee, and in the second, as many members of the congregation as possible. Arrange for child care and provide food if you do a congregational covenant meeting. It is good, as in the mission statement process, to personally call and invite every member of the congregation to participate. If your congregation is interested in developing a covenant, call your District Office. Remember, the more people who participate in the decision-making process, the greater the commitment to the outcome will be.

INTERNAL MANAGEMENT OF CONGREGATIONAL CONFLICT

The Unitarian Church of Victoria, British Columbia, did two more important things. They developed an internal "conflict management policy" and they appointed an internal conflict management team. Below are the key elements adapted from their conflict management policy and a description of the roles and responsibilities of a good congregational conflict management team.

CONFLICT MANAGEMENT POLICIES

This checklist can be useful when conflict arises; each person agrees to consider the following before proceeding:

- How willing am I to resolve this conflict?
- Do I want this to work for both of us or only for myself?
- What is the key issue or problem in this conflict?

- What do I want to change—and how do I say so without blame or attack?
- How well am I seeing the whole picture?
- Am I using power inappropriately? Is the other person?
- Am I judging the other person without hearing him or her?
- What are my feelings? Am I blaming him or her for my feelings?
- Have I told him or her how I feel?
- What would it be like to take the other person's position—to walk in their shoes?
- What do I wish to accomplish specifically?
- What can I give?
- What points would I need to have covered if we made an agreement?
- How can we all save face?
- Can we manage this ourselves or do we need outside help?
- What opportunities are present for our congregation in this conflict?
- How will we acknowledge and celebrate our solution?

Here is a congregational covenant or agreement from the Unitarian Church of Victoria:

> We are members of a religious community and intend to see our community thrive. Conflicts naturally occur between members; left unattended they will erode the trust and harmony necessary for our community's health. We therefore acknowledge a personal obligation to learn and practice ways of preventing and resolving conflicts promptly and successfully.
>
> As we perceive ourselves as a supportive and principled community, WE COVENANT: to treat each member with respect and to observe the Conflict Management Policy and Congregational Code of Good Relations adopted by this church.
>
> *Our policy:* To fulfill our covenant, each member will agree not to discredit motives, use offensive labels or other verbal abuse, spread malicious gossip, or threaten another person's welfare or church associations.

Further, if complaints or disagreements occur between members, they will attempt to resolve the problem between themselves. If they cannot, they shall follow the congregational Conflict Management Process.

Persons not involved in the specific conflict will communicate with others about the conflict only to initiate the Process.

Further, behavior in meetings will be facilitated by the chairperson. If arguments erupt and disrupt the meeting, the disputants will be asked to retract their statements or withdraw until they can participate respectfully. The request for withdrawal may be made by the chair or any member of the committee; in such circumstances withdrawal is obligatory.

Further, matters of uncontained conflict around issues of policy and / or ministry will be handled by an outside, neutral person, ombudsman, or other professional arbitrator, as suggested in the September, 1995, Pacific Northwest District CONTACT Team Report.

In cases as described in this last paragraph, it is prudent for the board to call the District Executive and discuss the options available within the district.

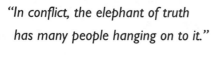

"In conflict, the elephant of truth has many people hanging on to it."

THE CONFLICT MANAGEMENT PROCESS

Each congregation needs to work out a conflict management process that the membership agrees on and to adopt it. You should develop recommendations about:

- how one member will interact with another
- how one member will interact with a group
- how the members of a group will interact
- how two or more groups will interact with each other
- how to proceed when the conflict involves board and minister
- how to proceed when the conflict involves board and staff
- how to proceed when the conflict involves minister and staff
- how to proceed when the conflict involves board and congregation
- how to proceed when the conflict involves minister and congregation
- whether the congregation wishes to appoint and train a conflict management team or an ombudsperson group
- when and by what authority the District or other outside consultants will be invited to intervene
- what conditions for removal from membership exist in the bylaws.

It is important to recommend the actions for adoption, implementation, and oversight of a conflict management process by the board when a conflict intervention report is written by an outside consultant.

The board of a congregation, in almost all cases, should not become the last court of appeal for a conflict. To do so puts them on the spot and in the middle of the conflict and they will too easily and often be seen as having chosen sides.

Outside intervention, a consultant from the district, or a local consultant, can provide a fair witness that impartially facilitates and helps manage the conflict.

The board of your congregation may wish to appoint a task force to meet with members of the congregation to assess and discuss congregational conflict policies and processes, then create a draft for the congregation's input and consideration. Following congregational input, the task force can incorporate suggestions and prepare a final draft to be formally adopted at a congregational meeting with a significant (75 percent or more) vote.

THE CONGREGATIONAL CONFLICT MANAGEMENT TEAM
OR OMBUDSPERSON GROUP

A group within your congregation—chosen, trained, and appointed by the board—can help prevent and manage conflict by doing many or one of the following:

- train the congregation in active listening skills
- provide information and suggestions for other kinds of skills training
- help people prepare for a meeting with someone with whom they have conflict
- meet with you and the other person and help work out a solution
- meet with two groups and assist in managing the conflict
- recommend when the board should seek outside help or intervention
- help to identify community resources for management
- organize conflict management workshops for congregational members
- report annually to the board and congregation.

"We do not need to think alike to love alike."

—FRANCIS DÁVID

Recruit a congregational Conflict Management Team that has strong skills in interpersonal communications, conflict management, group process, and facilitation. Ideally, members of this team would have the respect of the congregation and would not be seen as partisans of a faction within the congregation.

Many resources are available from your district, the Unitarian Universalist Association, and the outside world. Call your District Executive to discuss possibilities and options. Find out when district training is available and check with community sources to learn when local training is available.

MORE GOOD STUFF TO READ

Dinkmeyer, Don and Gary D. McKay. *Systematic Training for Effective Parenting.* Circle Pines, MN: American Guidance Service, Inc., 1997.

Haugk, Kenneth C. *Antagonists in the Church: How to Identify and Deal with Destructive Conflict.* Minneapolis, MN: Augsburg Publishing House, 1988. How to prevent or reduce much of the pain and suffering caused by antagonism and tell the difference between constructive, healthy conflict and destructive antagonism.

Leas, Speed B. *Leadership and Conflict*. Nashville, TN: Abingdon Press, 1982. Leas is a continentally known consultant on congregational conflict. The book is for those who are dealing with conflict: leaders, clergy, laity.

_____. *Moving Your Church Through Conflict*. Washington, DC: Alban Institute, 1985.

Washburn, Patricia and Robert Gribbon. *Peacemaking Without Division: Moving Beyond Congregational Apathy and Anger*. Bethesda, MD: Alban Institue, 1986. Advice for working with congregational groups on peacemaking issues.

CHAPTER TEN

Reproductive System

Every living organism has within it the potential for creativity.
Cells shed, yet the pattern renews itself.
They *transcend* themselves, creating new forms.
Living systems always, always, always
explore.
Grow.
Evolve.
Create.

Listen to this: Growth is not the objective. It is a sign, a symptom, and an indicator of a healthy congregation. As in flowers, trees, fish, birds, animals, and the children we adore, signs of growth are signs of good health. The garden grows and multiplies—and we flourish. Any living thing that ceases to grow begins to die. Just as we care for our gardens and pets, the creatures of the forest and field, and our children, our congregation must pay attention to its health.

Some people fear congregational growth, that things will change, that they will be different in their sweet, familiar church if it grows. They are right.

Just as a new baby turns the house upside down, just as life is never the same after its arrival, so a congregation changes irrevocably when it starts to grow. There are people you don't know around; the parking lot is full. You have to share power with new members. The newsletter gets thick with their names. The sanctuary begins to fill up each Sunday. There's more work to do; the budget is bigger, so you have to raise more money. The minister is busier. The building is used all the time.

That's the down side. The up side is that you meet and make new friends. You have two services to choose from. You share the leadership with new, energetic people. The newsletter has an editor and a new look. The sanctuary begins to fill up each Sunday. The leadership pool deepens, so there are more people to do the work. Financial resources increase; you can afford to increase staff hours. The building is used all the time and the future is exciting and wide open.

There are hundreds of thousands of people out there who could consider themselves part of us. Some even call themselves Unitarian Universalists. Who are these people? They are trying new spiritual paths and places and are looking to root, to rest, to nest, to come home. They were wounded by past church experiences. They want a place for their children to learn ethics and values and are seeking personal fulfillment, self actualization. They need to be wanted, useful, loved. They are testing, noisy, active, gay or lesbian or bisexual or straight, curious, explorers, seekers, justice seekers, and social change agents. They are ethnically, racially, and culturally diverse, in pain and lonely, sometimes difficult. They come from a range of economic circumstances, social classes, and educational levels; they desire friendship, affinity, and like-minded souls to be with. They have heard about us and hopefully, tentatively, come to our doors.

You probably have visitors every Sunday. Do they come back? Do they stay? If not, why not? Here are some of the most important things you can learn about growth: A congregation that does not want to grow will not grow. A congregation that is healthy and offers an environment for spiritual awakening cannot keep from growing. Which best describes your congregation?

Newcomers will join only if they feel they have found a spiritual home, a welcoming religious community. Will your congregation make sure they know that? It begins when your congregation makes a decision to attract and welcome new people.

GETTING READY TO GROW: HOW ATTRACTIVE ARE WE?

Ask yourself: Why did I join? What keeps me coming? Ask your congregation:

- Who are we? Do we welcome diversity? Are we people of color, of differing classes, gay and lesbian? Are we families with children? Single people? Older and younger? How diverse are the members of our congregation?

  Consider participating in the Welcoming Congregation program offered by the Unitarian Universalist Association.

- Do people in our congregation truly respect other points of view? Do some people put other people down or ridicule them? Can we debate issues and part friends?

  If you are not sure, or if you are sure and concerned, offer the What Do I Believe, What Do We Believe? Exercise from Chapter 2, "Breath and Spirit: Animating Congregational Life." Also try Listening Triads from Chapter 4, "Ears: Fostering Good Communications."

- Try having conversation groups to talk about differences, using the rule that the purpose of the group is to listen to, learn about, and respect the beliefs of others, rather than to promote one's own beliefs.

- Organize a year-long monthly discussion group for eight to ten people (have several) that meets in the evening with popcorn or over coffee and dessert. Choose a regular date, like the First Friday or Second Sunday. As a stimulus to discussion, view videos like PBS's *Bill Moyers Conversations* that are available for purchase. Develop a library of nine or ten of them, which can be circulated to different groups at different times. You can also obtain videos from the local library, or rent movies with ethical or religious themes. Choose challenging subjects like race, poverty, or gender. View them and talk about them afterwards, following these guidelines for listening: Let each person take a turn (have a timekeeper) to describe how they felt. Agree to ask questions that edify. Agree not to argue in hurtful, patronizing, or demeaning ways.

- Ask: Are we good caretakers? Do we love beauty? Does our property look cared for? Is our space ready to meet people? Will visitors say,

"Wow! What a neat place!?" If not, it's time to do a building audit and a "makeover." For how to do it, see Chapter 12, "Skin, Hair, Teeth, and Nails: Better, More Attractive Buildings."

- Ask: Do we enjoy our children? Are we an intergenerational community? If you have concerns, contact your District Office to ask for help, workshops, and conferences that enhance curriculum and religious education programs. You can get help starting religious education programs for children, youth, and adults.

- Ask: Do we sing a lot? Making a "joyful noise" is a wonderful thing. A congregation that loves to sing is a healthy congregation. Some do it naturally; for some it is a matter of practice.

  Meet a half hour before the service to learn hymns. Have a good song leader teach the hymns. Ask the Worship Committee or the Sunday Services Committee to choose a hymn of the month, and sing that hymn every Sunday of one month. Repeat for twelve months and you'll have a glorious repertoire of music.

- Ask: Do we break bread together? Preparing and sharing food together is a wonderful thing. Here are several ways to do it:

  Have a monthly after-the-service potluck. Or have "Wonderful Wednesday" or "Terrific Tuesday" potlucks, and have all congregational committees meet that night. Provide child care, serve dinner at six, and everyone is finished with meetings at nine o'clock. There can be a brief chapel for closing, too.

  Dinners for eight: put sign-up lists on the bulletin board with eight spaces for names. Recruit two people to be hosts the first time. People sign up for a dinner group and rotate hosting. The conversation is informal, the meal is around a table.

  Have a monthly 1960s-type coffeehouse during the winter months. Ask volunteers to bake fresh bread to serve with butter and honey. Supply chessboards. Offer an open mike for people to read poetry, play guitars, or sing. Put flowers and candies on the table. If you don't have a sound system, get a good boom box and play classical, folk, or New Age tapes, but not too loudly. Open it to young and old—people from 17 to 70. A different congregational group can sponsor it each month.

- Ask: Do we share our stories? If you don't have a program like this in place, see Chapter 8, "Heart: Creating and Nurturing Ministry."

- Ask: Do we work on conflict, rather than letting it go underground or accelerate? Do we have congregational agreement about what constitutes good and honorable relations in our congregations?

  A congregation that is fighting all the time, no matter the issue, is not a welcoming congregation. Every congregation needs to consider how it will handle its behavior and its differences. A Congregational Covenant is a good idea. If your congregation doesn't have one, see Chapter 9, "Liver: Dealing with Congregational Conflict."

- Ask: Do we really care about justice, equity, and compassion in human relations? What does our congregation do for others? Do we concentrate only on ourselves?

  A congregation that works only for itself faces inward. A congregation that has a commitment to social justice faces outward to the world. Most congregations are in between. If you want to learn more about your congregation and community and to identify opportunities for work on behalf of justice, see Chapter 6, "Feet: Public Relations and Evangelism."

- Ask: Do we have a clear congregational identity? A clear sense of mission?

  Look over Chapter 5, "Eyes: Developing a Congregational Future," and Chapter 6, "Feet: Public Relations and Evangelism." If your congregation has not revisited its mission during the last three years, it is time to do it again. Call your District Office for help or use the mission process in this book.

1. Keep a couple of UUA Principles and Purposes wallet cards handy. If anyone asks you what your congregation is about, you can give them one. Buy a supply from the Unitarian Universalist Association Bookstore for people in your congregation to use.

2. Have a workshop on "What do you say after you say you're a Unitarian Universalist?" Repeat the workshop on four consecutive weeks (a different evening each week) so that many members can come. Divide into pairs. Have each pair create a situation in which they can imagine themselves being asked that question. Role play the responses.

3. Invite people to come and visit. Seventy-four percent of people who come to a congregation for the first time do so because someone in that congregation asked them. Think about saying to a friend, a coworker, or a new neighbor: "Have you found a congregation yet? If not, you might be interested in my congregation. Why don't you come next Sunday? I'll pick you up."

4. Reserve a few parking spaces near the door for visitors. Make sure there are clear directions from the parking lot to the door. Be sure that the building is accessible (including bathrooms and all floors) and that there is a handicapped parking space. If newcomers with special needs arrive, be sure greeters are prepared to welcome and guide them in.

5. Make sure the front door is open, attractive, and welcoming. Have greeters at the door, including a greeter to take children and parents to religious education.

6. Being a greeter is a great volunteer task for new members. They know how it is to visit without knowing anyone. Because they have just joined, they are excited and have valuable suggestions about how to welcome and include newcomers.

7. Have a name tag, a visitor's packet, and an order of service ready for newcomers. Ask them to sign a visitor's book, which should record whether they wish to receive the newsletter. Put visitors on the newsletter mailing list for at least six months. The visitor's

packet should contain information about the Unitarian Universalist Association, your district, and your congregation, including religious education and program information. The packet should give them lots of well-presented information about your religious community.

8. Have a welcome table in the foyer of your building that is easily visible from the door. Be sure it is attractive and inviting: Put a cloth, flowers, literature, and visitor's packets on it. Have a warm, knowledgeable member of the Membership Committee or other volunteers, staff the table.

9. See that there are floaters available to sit with visitors. Find resident extroverts and ask them to wear large, bright name tags. Ask them to stand up at the beginning of the service and tell everyone that they want to talk to visitors.

10. Give visitors a pew card to fill out and drop in the collection plate. A pew card lists congregational activities and provides boxes for visitors to check areas that interest them. It asks for their comments and whether they wish to hear from the minister or a member of the congregation.

11. Ask greeters and floaters to personally invite newcomers to coffee hour and to escort them there, introducing them to other people who may share their interests.

12. If you use different, special coffee cups for newcomers, be certain you go and talk with them.

13. Have a board rotation list for coffee hour, so that one or two board members have the responsibility to talk to new people each Sunday.

14. Have a newcomer's table in the room where you hold coffee hour, with someone to staff it. Find out what interests each person who visits it and introduce them to someone who is in the area.

15. Make a congregational rule: No church business during the first 20 minutes of coffee hour. That's the best time to greet and get acquainted with newcomers. If you can't make it an all-church rule, make it a rule for the Membership Committee, the board, and all committee chairs.

16. Introduce visitors to the minister. The minister can host a monthly meeting after the service in her or his office with coffee and cookies. Put up a poster to announce the event so people know about it. Have staff at the visitor's table announce when it is happening: "Our minister is having a special welcome in the Minister's Study today. If you have questions about us, or would just like to get acquainted with her (him), please come. It begins 15 minutes after the service."

17. Call first-time visitors within 72 hours of their visit. Studies show that a warm, non-intrusive phone call will increase the probability by 50 percent that visitors will come back. Recruit someone to make these calls who is knowledgeable, warm, and comfortable on a telephone. Have them say something like: "I'm Joan Smith from the East Cupcake UU Congregation. We are so glad you came to visit us! I'm calling to see if you have any questions I can answer, and if not, to just say hello and that we hope to see you again! (If you can't answer a question, say that you will get back to them with the answer, then do it.)

18. Ask the minister to send a follow-up note one week after a first-time visit, saying, "I'm glad you chose to visit us. Please call me or introduce yourself next time if you have questions. I look forward to meeting you."

19. When newcomers come again, greet them by name. If, at the end of six months, visitors don't know and are not known by at least six people, they probably won't return.

20. Ask visitors if they are interested in joining. Some people wait for your invitation; some people just don't think about it.

SO THEY'RE INTERESTED IN MEMBERSHIP

Newcomers should learn what membership in a congregation means. What do prospective members need to know to make a decision to join? What are, as Dean Kelley puts it, "the minimum maxims of seriousness?"

NEW MEMBER CLASSES

Every congregation should offer new member orientation classes. Some congregations call them "New Unitarian Universalist" classes. Here prospective members can learn about Unitarian Universalism, its history and structure, and its Principles and Purposes. They can learn about their district and the learning and leadership development opportunities it offers. They also can learn about congregational polity, which is so important to Unitarian Universalism.

New member classes are the best place to talk about your congregation. New members, in addition to learning about the larger Unitarian Universalist community, should learn the history, the mission, the covenant, and the requirements of membership in your congregation and any expectations about congregational conduct (see Chapter 9, "Liver: Dealing with Congregational Conflict"). They will of course want to know about members' rights and responsibilities. Here are some questions you should be prepared to answer:

- What do I get for my membership?
- Do I have to sign anything?
- Do I have to agree to believe in something? If so, what?
- How much money do I have to pay?
- Do I have to agree to work for the church? How often?
- What does the congregation offer a member—or a friend?
- What kinds of activities are there?
- Are there different categories of membership?

New member classes can be conducted as a one-day session, all day on a Saturday, a series of two-hour evening meetings over a period of weeks, or a combination of the above. Usually the minister and a board member conduct these classes together. You may wish to invite your district board member or Unitarian Universalist Association trustee to drop in briefly, if they are within reasonable distance.

The religious educator should talk about congregational religious education opportunities for children, youth, and adults.

The chair of the pledge drive should speak candidly about the cost—to the congregation—of its members and about sharing financial responsibility.

Every member is a steward of the congregation and has stewardship responsibilities. Every member should have the opportunity to give. New members should be advised that they will be canvassed within six weeks of joining. Interestingly, new members as a group give more generously than ongoing members, so take advantage of this early opportunity to expand the stewardship of your congregation.

Each year your congregation gets a new "class" of members—those who joined during that church year. Some mid-sized and larger congregations invite each year's class to choose and accomplish a service project for the building: painting a room, planting a garden, getting the library re-organized. This gives the new members a feeling of physical involvement and commitment to their new religious community.

BUILDING COMMITMENT

There are many ways to build the level of commitment of your newest members.

- Give every new member an opportunity to meet with the minister personally and have an interview. This will allow the minister to get to know newer members individually and give members the opportunity to feel comfortable with the minister. Getting to know the minister allows the minister to be more accessible in times of crisis.
- Offer new member classes two or three times a year.
- Plan a new member ingathering one to three times a year. Ingatherings are the time when the congregation and the minister formally welcome new members into the community. Plan the event for fall, winter, and spring, so that newcomers know when they will have an opportunity to join. The ingathering should be a part of the Sunday morning service.

INGATHERING DAY

This is a special day for new members and the congregation.

- Announce in the newsletter and the orders of service preceding the ingathering that new members will be welcomed into the congregation on a particular date.

- Extend a special invitation to the new members, requesting their presence on that Sunday to be welcomed into the congregation.
- Prepare the room to make the sanctuary especially festive that morning.
- Talk to the music director and the minister, so that you will be singing hymns that are about community, such as hymn #360, "Here We Have Gathered"; hymn #1, "May Nothing Evil Cross This Door"; hymn #361, "Enter, Rejoice, and Come In"; or hymn #389, "Gathered Here." (See *Singing the Living Tradition.*) Usually, an ingathering takes place toward the beginning of the service.
- When the time comes, ask new members to come to the front of the room. Call out each name. Pat Kridler, membership director of the First Unitarian Society of Minneapolis, liked to find out something special about each person and tell it to the congregation: "This fall's class of members includes a geophysicist, a woman who built her own house, the 1978 Popcorn Queen of Texas, a man who speaks three languages, a couple who honeymooned on the Muir Trail, and a bookbinder."

  Pat never told anyone who was who, so the congregation was always challenged to try to find out at coffee hour. This is especially effective in larger congregations.

  Some congregations like to have a current member interview and introduce each new member. This works best when membership classes are small. If you have more than four new members, it can get lengthy.
- Plan a ceremony of commitment. The president or moderator of the congregation should lead the ceremony. Here is a sample:

PRESIDENT: The Unitarian Universalist Congregation of the Prairies would like to welcome you this joyful morning. We are a community of friendship and purpose. You have learned about us and the Unitarian Universalist Association of Congregations. You have made the important decision to enter into membership. We celebrate that decision and invite you this day to covenant with us.

NEW MEMBERS: I make a commitment to uphold the Unitarian Universalist Association Principles and Purposes and the covenant of this congregation. I will try to live these values in my daily life. I will be present to walk with you in the search for truth and understanding. I will be intentional about my own lifelong growth and learning. I will share the work of this congregation by giving of such time and talents as I can and I will support our mutual effort of stewardship with a pledge. To the best of my ability, I will be a model for our children, a mentor for our youth, and a friend to those in need.

CONGREGATION: We receive you with open hands and hearts. As you join us, we once again renew our own commitment to this religious community. We are proud to have you among us. Welcome. Welcome. Welcome!

- A board reception for new members can be held at the home of a board member or another member of the congregation, or at the church. It is more intimate and friendlier to have the reception in a home. This is a simple evening, with coffee, tea, and finger food. Once everyone has arrived, invite people to sit down. The entire board should be present and one member can invite everyone to talk one by one about how they found the congregation and why they joined. Keep official welcoming speeches to a minimum, but have them from the minister and the board president. Allow a time for socializing afterwards. The event will take about two hours.

GERMINATION: GETTING NEW MEMBERS INVOLVED

A skills interest survey is one effective way to find out the interests of new members. If you have a computer, the information can be entered into your database. Here is a sample:

NAME _____ PHONE NUMBER _____
ADDRESS _____
CITY _____ STATE _____ ZIP _____

Please circle those areas of congregational life which interest you most. Please place a check mark next to those you would like to know more about:

WORSHIP AND CELEBRATION
___ Sanctuary (foyer) Art Gallery
___ Music Committee
___ Choir
___ Sunday Service (or Worship) Committee
___ Flowers
___ Ushers
___ Greeters

SOCIAL JUSTICE
___ Social Justice Committee
___ Food Closet
___ Prison Volunteers
___ Habitat for Humanity Group
___ Meals for the Homeless
___ Adopt a River Project

PASTORAL AND MINISTRY
___ Caring Committee
___ Visitors
___ Lay Ministers
___ Meals for the Homebound
___ Transportation on Sunday mornings
___ Grantwriting Group

MEMBERSHIP
___ Membership Committee
___ Welcomers

___ Newsletter
___ Public Relations Committee
___ Publications Task Force

STEWARDSHIP
___ Finance Committee
___ Financial Planning Group
___ Congregational Budget Committee
___ Investments Committee
___ Annual Pledge Canvass Service
___ Special Events
___ Auction Night
___ Capital Campaign Committee

RELIGIOUS EDUCATION
___ Religious Education
___ Youth Adult Committee
___ Teenage Advisor
___ Adult Religious Education Committee
___ Nursery
___ Teaching Religious Education
___ Planning Intergenerational Events
___ Library Committee
___ Archives and History Committee

BUILDING AND GROUNDS
___ Building Committee
___ Grounds Committee
___ Aesthetics Committee
___ Maintenance Planning Committee

GOVERNANCE
___ Long-range Planning Committee
___ Personnel Committee
___ Board

___ Bylaws Committee
___ Leadership Development Committee

OTHER

WELCOMERS

"Welcomers" is one name for a group of people charged with personally contacting new members for a face-to-face interview. They perform the same function as a skills inventory, but more personally. The Welcomer calls up Ms. and Mr. Newmember, inviting them to meet at a local coffeehouse. The Welcomer listens and finds out what this couple cares about, why they joined, how they would like to join in the life of the congregation. If Ms. Newmember likes to sing and Mr. Newmember is a social activist, the Welcomer sees that Ms. gets called by the choir director and invited to join the choir, and that Mr. is invited to a Social Justice Committee meeting. These calls should be made within a week of meeting the new members.

Each Welcomer does no more than six interviews each year. Welcomers are selected because they are good listeners, adept at drawing people out, and fun to talk to. They should be chosen, because not everyone is good at it. The minister and the membership chair might get together to make a list of potential Welcomers.

SOCIAL PARTICIPATION

In addition to the skills interest survey and a call from a Welcomer, here are some tried and true ways to get people involved. Socializing is a must for newcomers: They need to get to know people, to feel welcome. It is important to ask people what they want to do not what you need them to do. The big secret to getting people involved is to find out what they are dying to do and to see that they get to do it.

- *New member potlucks:* New member classes, particularly with six or more people, enjoy having potlucks two or three times a year. They can develop friendships with each other in addition to entering the rest of congregational life. Some new member classes still hold annual potlucks five years after they became members.

- *A first anniversary party for new members:* Interview new members about their first year's experience. An anniversary party is a great way to do it. The Membership Committee can throw the party and midway through have people sit down and talk about how entering into this congregation has been. Easy? Difficult? Why? What do they wish they were getting that they are not getting? What works, what's fun, what's engaging?

- *Fireside chats:* Here is a way for the minister to get better acquainted with the members of a congregation. Fireside chat conversations should be freewheeling, with no formal agenda other than inviting people to introduce themselves and share how they found out about Unitarian Universalism and came to visit this congregation for the first time.

  Continuing members, visitors, and new members should be included in the invitation to a chat. Here's how it works: Post a sign-up list, one a month for every month of the "fireside season" (say, October through March), prominently on the bulletin board. Include ten lines and two additional lines for alternates to write their names and addresses. Announce the chats in the newsletter and the order of service:

  > Fireside Chats with our minister, Jim Warmly, will begin on October 4 and will be held throughout the winter on November 7, December 5, January 10, February 2, and March 9. Sign-up sheets are on the bulletin board in the Social Hall. They will be held at Reverend Warmly's home from 7 to 9 P.M. and will be informal, fun, and a way to meet your fellow members. Coffee, tea, and cookies will be served. Only ten people per chat, so sign up soon.

  Send a reminder postcard to participants about a week before the chat. If possible, invite the alternates anyway, if there is room.

Some ministers like to have a monthly gathering at a local café, always choosing the same day and the same meal, like breakfast the first Tuesday, or lunch the second Wednesday of the month. They list it regularly in the newsletter:

> Breakfast with Barbara. First Tuesdays of the month at the Coffee House Café, at 7:30 A.M. Anyone who wishes may come by and enjoy breakfast or a cup of coffee and conversation with our minister.

- *Zip Code Groups:* Hold social gatherings for everyone in the same zip code. Be sure to combine adjoining zip codes if there are fewer people in one code than another. Zip Code Groups can have potlucks or holiday gatherings. They are sometimes effectively used as focus groups to discuss important issues on the congregational agenda.

- *Circle suppers* are a tried and true way to socialize in small groups several times a year. (Sometimes called "Dinner for Eight.") Usually organized by sign-up sheets on the bulletin board after host families have been recruited.

- *Physical Activity Groups:* Many people like to find ways to exercise with other people. Congregations can offer hiking, biking, skiing, canoeing, tai chi, yoga, early morning walking, country and western line dancing, contra dancing, folk dancing, kayaking, rowing, and aerobic exercise.

- *4x4x4 Dinners:* Here is a way to meet people in or out of your congregation whom you might not ordinarily meet. Fear, or phobia, is most often based on not knowing the "other." A 4x4x4 dinner gives us an opportunity to get acquainted. Organize these dinners through sign-up sheets, with advance notices in the newsletter and announcements from the pulpit on Sunday morning. The first "4" symbolizes participants who commit themselves to four dinners during the church year. The second "4" represent four members of the congregation who are heterosexual. The third "4" are four members of the congregation who are gay, lesbian, or bisexual. (Or the second "4" can be members of your congregation, such as older teenagers, and the third "4" can be members of another congregation with a different racial, ethnic, or religious mix.)

- *Attending services:* All members, not just new members, should be encouraged to attend services. The Sunday morning service is at the center of congregational life. Someone once said, "I try to go to church every Sunday, even when I don't feel like it, because I look forward to seeing people I know and love there. I feel disappointed when they don't come—I wish they had. So I try not to disappoint others. That's one good reason I attend regularly."

- *Volunteer activity booklets:* A volunteer activity booklet, which describes all the opportunities for involvement, says to new members, "We want you to be an active part of our congregation. Here are the ways you can do that." A useful activity booklet will include a letter

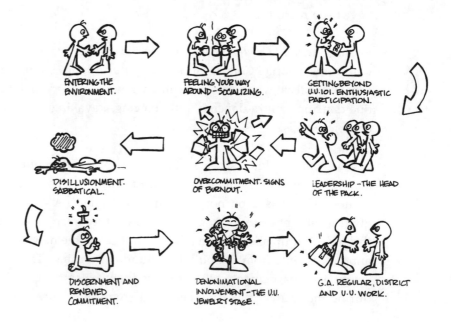

from the minister and/or board president inviting participation, a table of contents, social activities, volunteer opportunities, committees and task forces, religious education programs and classes for adults (a separate booklet should describe programs for children and youth), social justice opportunities, congregational events (including the annual meeting), a congregational calendar, a registration form for classes, and names and phone numbers of contact people for each committee or event.

CONGREGATIONAL GROWTH

If your congregation is open and inclusive, diverse and engaging, creative and fun; if it's moving and growth-producing and caring, people will beat their way to your door.

That means growth and growth means change and both of these things can be scary. It's hard to know what your congregation will be like if it grows. It is good to talk about growth and change and to consider their effects. Larry Peers of the UUA Department of District, Congregational, and Extension Services offers three important questions about growth and change:

- If our church grows significantly, what changes do we anticipate?
- Will church growth seriously change our identity or our mission?
- What would our church be like without significant growth?

This last question is important for at least two reasons. First, like any living thing, a congregation that ceases to grow begins to die. If you are in a small, comfortable congregation that likes things the way they are, look around and consider: Who will be here when we are gone? Do we exist for ourselves only? Second, congregations that turn inward and don't look out beyond their doors should ask themselves: What if this congregation were not here when I needed it? What if they didn't want me to belong?

Six hours

Newsprint

Water-based markers

Masking tape

Two sheets of butcher paper,
4' x 6' and 4' x 8'

Adhesive dots, three for each
person

Cassette player and tapes

Information packet for each

Name tags

Bell or bowl

Coffee, tea, and water

Finger foods

Lunch prepared by someone
other than congregational
members

Chalice

Tape the two sheets of butcher
paper to separate walls. On the
4' x 8' sheet, write a long-range
planning graph using these
headings: Goal A, Objective 1,
Action Step A, Accountability,
By When. Prepare name tags

CONGREGATIONAL GROWTH PLAN DAY

The following process is a half-day, all-congregation workshop called Congregational Growth Plan Day. Provide child care, a check-in table, and refreshments. Have the child-care providers arrive early. They should not be members of the congregation so arrange for a trade off with a neighboring congregation. Make the same trade-off arrangements for lunch.

Start the process by asking yourself: Does our congregation have a mission and a vision? Having a strong sense of mission and a clearly defined vision enhances congregational growth and draws people in. A vision and mission statement helps answer questions such as, "Do we really want to grow? How large do we want to be in five years? What do we value? What do we want to be and do in the world?"

If your congregation does not have a mission and vision, look at Chapter 5, "Eyes: Developing a Congregational Future," and self-facilitate the process or call your District Office to find an outside facilitator. If you have a mission and vision, find out when they were written. Mission statements need to be revisited every three to five years because most congregations' membership changes significantly during that time. Everyone should be excited about and committed to the mission.

After determining your congregation's mission and vision, prepare to answer the following questions. You should have the Membership Committee and the Annual Pledge Drive Committee gather this information well in advance of Growth Plan Day. It will help everyone understand the dynamics and resources of your congregation.

- What is the average Sunday-morning attendance of your congregation? (Average every Sunday over a two-month period.)
- What is your religious education enrollment and the average religious education attendance on Sundays?
- What is your current adult membership?
- What does your congregation require for membership?
- What is the average pledge per pledging unit in your congregation? Are people making pledges to a Capital Campaign as well? What is that average pledge? What is the distribution of pledges?

- What active committees exist in your congregation?
- What is your congregation's current path to membership? List entry points and affinity groups (social groups, committees, clubs) for the assimilation of newcomers.
- What is the general population and what are the demographics of your congregation's area? How are you publicizing your congregation?
- Do you have a building? Is it clean, attractive, accessible, and functional? Is there adequate space for Sunday attendance and your religious education program?

for participants by dividing them into small groups and drawing symbols for the respective groups.

Ask your board to schedule the workshop. Ask it to appoint a planning committee to ensure that the workshop is presented effectively and on time. If the committee needs help, have it call your District Office to suggest an outside facilitator. If you use an inside facilitator, be sure it is a person with significant group process skills. Here's a checklist:

____ Reserve adequate meeting space for the entire attending group.

____ Be sure the meeting space has enough breakout space for small groups, one space for every eight participants.

____ Arrange for free child care for the entire day.

____ Arrange to have a noon meal catered and cleaned up by someone other than members. (A neighboring congregation may be willing to trade.)

____ Send personal invitations (a letter from the president or moderator, signed by the minister, too) to every member. Follow up with a personal phone call from a board or committee member, urging people to attend because their input is important.

____ Plan advance publicity. Put an article and a notice in the newsletter. Put an announcement in the order of service each Sunday four weeks beforehand.

____ Put posters on the bulletin board six weeks in advance.

____ Make pulpit announcements every Sunday for one month in advance.

At least half of the congregation should be present for the workshop. If not enough people commit themselves to coming, that tells you something important about their interest in growth. If this is the case, the board may want to discuss it and plan what to do to inspire interest. Reschedule the event for the following year or half-year.

Have the board appoint a Growth-Plan Follow-up Committee. This committee should be composed of members who attended the workshop and will be responsible for seeing that what the congregation wants gets done.

Review the differences—or produce a glossary of the differences—between mission, vision, covenant, and values. Make copies of your congregation's mission, covenant, and vision for each person present. Compile all this information to be distributed in a packet for all participants.

Opening

Play music as people arrive. Call them to the opening with a bell or bowl. Choose a reading from *Singing the Living Tradition* such as #490, "Wild Geese." Light the chalice. Welcome people and explain the purpose of the day. Example: "Welcome to the first Congregational Growth Workshop of the Unitarian Universalist Society of the Plains. It is wonderful that so many of us are here, participating in planning for and building our future. Today we will dream a bit, and then make concrete plans to bring into being."

Historical Timeline

The six-foot sheet of butcher paper is for a historical timeline. When the attitudes of a congregation inhibit growth, it is useful to allow people to explore their feelings about growth. Doing a historical timeline puts the life of the congregation into perspective and facilitates this process.

Draw a horizontal line down the middle of the butcher paper. Put the name of the congregation on the top of the page. Put the year the congregation was founded on the far left side and the current year on the far right side. Ask people to identify major events in the life of the congregation, important dates, important issues, watershed events, ministers and their eras. Record these on the top half of the paper. On the bottom half, ask people to identify (then record) congregational heroes, myths and stories about the congregation, and traditions and rituals.

Invite participants to study the page for a few minutes. Ask them what they have learned and what observations they make about themselves. Record those on separate sheets of newsprint.

Brainstorm

Explain that within the current context of congregational life you'd like to challenge them to brainstorm. Use two sheets of paper and two pens of different colors. On one sheet ask them to brainstorm the inhibitors to membership growth in your congregation: What things—staffing, leadership, activities or the lack of them, facilities, and customs—might keep you from growing? On the second sheet, brainstorm the enhancers: What things—staffing, leadership, activities, facilities, customs—will help you grow?

Produce both lists by the same brainstorm—use one color pen on one sheet, the second color pen on the second sheet. Or use two people as recorders, one working in each category. Examples: not enough hymnals, inadequate religious education space, no parking *or* great people, charming building, good social programs, etc.

Guided Meditation

This guided meditation uses an exercise from Chapter 5, "Eyes: Developing a Congregational Future" called Congregational Vision. Ask participants to silently imagine their most exciting vision for five years from now. Following the meditation, ask them to divide into small groups according to the symbol on their name tag. Ask them to listen to small group instructions first, then proceed to the breakout room for their group. Give each group a piece of newsprint and a marker. Ask them to appoint one person to record and report back to the large group. Give them 30 to 40 minutes to list the elements of their vision, note those that were mentioned frequently, and come up with a group vision that they record on newsprint. Remind them that this is a consensual process, which means that everyone can live with the results, not that every person must be in complete agreement with every item.

You may wish to play soft classical or New Age music during this meditation. Practice reading the meditation out loud, not too slow and not too fast while the music is playing, ahead of time. If the music seems disruptive, do not use it. If you use music, fade it in and out, as the abrupt change of the stop button can be jarring.

Start the guided meditation.

When the guided meditation is finished, say, "You may now proceed to your small group spaces. Let each person have a turn sharing their growth vision, then develop a vision for your group. We will meet again here in 35 minutes."

Putting It All Together

After a brief break when everyone has returned to the large group, ask each small group's recorder to report on their vision. Post the results on the walls. After each group has reported, invite the large group to look at the postings in silence for a minute or two, noticing the commonalities. Ask them which items appear the most frequently and if any items appear on all groups' visions. The elements mentioned most often should become prospective goals for your Congregational Growth Plan.

Provide each participant with three adhesive dots and invite everyone to place one dot per item on each of their top three choices for congregational priorities. The three items with the most dots can become the three congregational growth plan goals.

Remind people that planning is a continual process—a work in progress—and that once a goal is accomplished, a new goal can replace it. Everything does not have to be accomplished in one year, and two or three goals are plenty to manage for a two- or three-year period.

Circle the final goals. Explain to people that each goal should be specific, attainable, and measurable (SAM). If the goals seem unclear or amorphous, ask the groups for clarification.

Divide the large group into three working groups, one for each goal. Using the eight-foot butcher paper as a model, ask each group to develop the objectives, action steps, accountabilities, and time line for their goal. What will need to be done for the congregation to accomplish that goal? Who will be responsible and by when? Here is an example:

> **Goal A:** The Unitarian Universalist Church of the Plains will improve and invigorate its newcomer and visitor welcoming program.
>
> Objective 1: The Membership Committee will appoint a task force to develop a visitors' program.
>
> Accountability: Membership Committee
> By when: May meeting

Action Step A: Task Force appointed, meets, goes to District Extension training.

Will develop a plan at training to take back to congregation by August.

Action Step B: Task Force, with Membership Committee, will have plan in place and ready to go by opening Sunday in September. (Greeter program, visitors' packet, visitors' table, resident extroverts, board member rotation for coffee hour, etc.)
Accountability: Task Force and Membership Committee
By when: September, opening Sunday.

Objective 2: Evaluate plan mid-year to determine use for following years.

Accountability: Task Force, Membership Committee
By when: March

Action Step A: Develop evaluation format. Contact all visitors, whether they have become members or not, and interview them about their experiences with the congregation.

Accountability: Task Force has oversight of evaluation
By when: March

Action Step B: Collate evaluations, write report
Accountability: Task Force
By when: Early April

Action Step C: Make recommendations to Membership Committee for revision and/or the continuation of visitor program
Accountability: Task Force
By when: May

Have each working group post and describe its plan to accomplish its goal.

Publicize by putting an article in the church newsletter about the Congregational Growth Plan day and the goals it developed. Post them on the bulletin board. At a congregational meeting, formally adopt the new plan, so that the whole congregation buys in. You should have a supermajority (2/3 or more) to adopt the plan.

Your District Office may have other ways of helping you look at growth. Perhaps they have consultants and facilitators for this purpose. Perhaps the Unitarian Universalist Association will offer a growth workshop for your size of congregation in your area.

One year later, check off and celebrate your accomplishments. Have a party. Celebrate these accomplishments with the congregation at worship or a special event or time.

TWO SERVICES OR A NEW BUILDING?

When you really begin to grow, you may begin to feel crowded. Generally, if you are consistently 85 percent full on Sunday mornings, you need to consider other options, such as having two services, remodeling, or finding another building. Any of these choices will enable you to reach out to the unchurched who are seeking a liberal religious community. Two services, for instance, allow current members to participate in familiar forms of worship while making room for others. New people have new energy and new ideas, too.

If you have this challenging but happy dilemma, your congregation should have many long, hard, discussions about what to do. Focus groups to discuss the alternatives are often a good way to go: They provide an opportunity to talk more deeply in small groups about choices. Eventually, the whole congregation will need to decide at a congregational meeting what to do. Your District Office has suggestions about how to design and facilitate this process.

A NEW MODEL FOR UNITARIAN UNIVERSALIST CONGREGATIONS

Larry Peers offers the following characteristics of a new model for Unitarian Universalist congregations. How does your congregation stand? Are you a congregation of the future? Are you:

- Mission focused
- Intentionally focused on spiritual growth
- A group that knows its surrounding community
- Clear about your ministry focus groups
- Offering outreach that is intentional and coordinated within your congregation's programs
- A congregation with cell groups
- A congregation with responsive program development
- Intentional with an ongoing shared ministry program
- Able to reach out to and serve diverse populations
- Anti-racist and multicultural
- Exercising responsible stewardship
- Using a mission budget process
- In "association" and covenant relationships with other Unitarian Universalist congregations
- Engaged with other faith communities in common social ministries, advocacy, and service?

Few congregations are all of these things. But this is a list of goals to strive for that reflect and represent Unitarian Universalist principles and purposes.

TWENTY WAYS TO NURTURE RELIGIOUS GROWTH

CHILDREN

1. Be sure that every religious education program nurtures awe and wonder.
2. Build self-esteem in religious education—children can't be affirmed too much.
3. Be clear about boundaries in religious education classrooms and intergenerational settings. It is not kind to children to let them run amuck.
4. Be sure children are making friends in religious education classes and the larger congregational community.
5. Ask children to write a credo (what I believe) each year. Save them

and present them when they come of age or are moving away.

6. Develop coming-of-age ceremonies for youth, at puberty and when entering adulthood. Find out about bridging and coming-of-age ceremonies from your District Office.

7. Celebrate rites of passage. When children have birthdays or special achievements, put it in the newsletter. Send them a card from the congregation.

8. Learn about the Sunday mornings that kids remember. Ask them to share: What's your earliest positive memory of a Sunday service? Negative?

9. Adults in the community define boundaries and model behavior for children. Remember, "It takes a village to raise a child."

10. Discuss the relationship between freedom and responsibility. How do they conflict? How are they complimentary?

11. "Service is our prayer" say the covenants of many congregations. Kids can do service projects, too. Ask each class to choose and do one service project each year.

12. Children need to learn about Unitarian Universalist identity. Where and how are the children in your congregation learning this?

13. There are many great Unitarian Universalist curricula: *Neighboring Faiths, Stepping Stone Year, Special Times, Rainbow Children, Celebrating Me and My World*—call your District Office or the Unitarian Universalist Association Bookstore to find out about what's new and available.

14. Teenagers can learn about their roots and branches, too. They can make a video about the congregation's history and interview elders, church leaders, former ministers, etc.

15. Kids love to learn about famous Unitarian Universalists. One minute of each Sunday school class can be dedicated to one famous Unitarian Universalist.

16. Explore LIFT (*Life Issues for Teenagers*).

17. Try a cycle for teens that consists of: nature-based and tribal religions; world religions; Christianity, Judaism, the development of Unitarian Universalism; and ethics.

18. Adolescence is a time to be challenged. See if members of your

congregation or district know how to offer vision quests, wilderness challenges, and service projects that involve physical work.

19. Be sure your congregation offers plenty of social opportunities for teens through YRUU or otherwise.

20. When your teenagers become young adults, invite them into real power. Recruit them to committees. Encourage them to become active in every area of congregational life.

ADULTS

1. Be sure your congregation offers a dynamic, diverse adult education program and an attractive brochure that lists all the courses for fall, winter, and spring.

2. Try creating 52 historic Sundays, devoting one or two minutes each Sunday to a famous Unitarian Universalist or event in Unitarianism or Universalism.

3. Offer adult religious education courses in Unitarian Universalist history, polity, and organization.

4. Explore and expand your theology/philosophy by offering credo writing groups or a Building Your Own Theology course. Encourage members to articulate their own beliefs at forums, talkbacks, or discussion groups.

5. Offer a course in personal ethics—how to live our ethics daily.

6. Sample devotional practices and spiritual practices. Develop spiritual growth groups, using Bill Houff's *Infinity in Your Hand*.

7. A lot of people—even Unitarian Universalists—want to know more about the Bible. Consider a series of conversations about the Bible, an Introduction to the Bible class, or Bible classes. Humanists might like to read the Bible as literature, followed by other great religious texts. Bill Moyers's *Genesis* series is wonderful; listening to one audio cassette, followed by coffee and conversation, makes for a great evening.

8. Hold an early Sunday morning Zen meditation group. James Ishmael Ford, a Unitarian Universalist minister, has written a book called *This Very Moment: A Brief Introduction to Buddhism and Zen for*

Unitarian Universalists. Perhaps a church member who is Buddhist or a member of a local Buddhist group can come and lead you.

9. Dream groups are wonderful. Unitarian Universalist minister Jeremy Taylor has written two excellent books on dreams and the meaning of dreaming. Start a dream group by reading one of them, or invite him to do a workshop and start a dream group from the workshop.

10. Offer chaplaincy or lay ministry training. Ask your minister and District Office to explore training offered by other congregations or to develop one.

11. Honor the concept of spiritual discipline and direction. Keep a journal about your own spiritual, or theological, or ethical direction. Get a group together to discuss it.

12. Some congregations have performance dance or movement groups at Sunday services. If you are a dancer, talk to your minister or worship committee about organizing one. Or form a theater group, choose a play, and offer it to the congregation as a fundraiser or in a Sunday morning service.

13. Consider having a mentor program. Match people in the congregation who have wisdom to share with learners.

14. Have a support group for commitment to the religious life: ethical behavior, justice making, the notion of practice, right relationship.

15. Produce video oral histories of the congregation's leaders and ministers through the years. Have a showing. Invite the youth—or let the youth produce them.

16. Study other religious traditions—visit other groups at their synagogues, mosques, and churches.

17. Some congregations use Bill Moyers's *A World of Ideas: Conversations with Thoughtful Men and Women about American Life Today and Ideas for Shaping Our Future* as the basis for a monthly discussion group: View *A World of Ideas* and follow it with your own conversation over a cup of coffee.

18. The Evergreen congregation in Marysville, Washington, has a *Star Trek* theology group. View the episode of *Star Trek*, talk about it afterwards.

19. Have a religious movie series. Gather in someone's home to view one movie a month, have popcorn, and socialize and talk afterwards. Good religious movies: *Resurrection, Dead Man Walking, Do the Right Thing, Ground Hog Day, Little Buddha, Defending Your Life, Grand Canyon, Strangers in Good Company, Stand and Deliver, Like Water for Chocolate, Contact.*

20. Honor, support, and affirm the oldest members of your congregation. Have a special Sunday each spring to acknowledge their contributions by making a few of them Honorary Members (who don't need to pledge), delivering a sermon on aging, and singing hymn #103, "For All the Saints." Give them a corsage or lapel flower. Seat them in front. Invite two or three (give them a time limit, like three minutes) to share how the congregation was when they first came to it. Arrange transportation for those who need it.

WHEN PEOPLE LEAVE

Just as people arrive in your congregation for all sorts of reasons, they also leave: The service isn't right for them; there is no religious education program; they didn't make friends; they are moving; they want their Sundays for themselves; they've had a disagreement with another member or group in the congregation.

EXIT INTERVIEWS

You'll never know why people leave unless you ask them. Suggest that your Membership Committee do exit interviews. An exit interview works best with a personal visit or phone call. The purpose is not to convince people of anything; rather, it is to find out their positive and negative experiences with the congregation. What worked for them, was attractive about the church? What caused them to decrease or stop attending; what put them off or was difficult? The Membership Committee should share the information with the board and minister and together plan changes that might be suggested by the results of the interviews.

SAYING GOOD-BYE

It is just as important to say good-bye, to have closure with departing members, as it is to say hello to them. Here are some ways to help make good, healthy farewells possible.

- Ask the minister or a board member to make a formal farewell call.
- A letter from the board president to the departing member should acknowledge their removal from membership, say their gifts will be missed, and wish them well.
- Ask the minister or board president to write a letter to the minister of their next church if the departing members are moving out of town. The letter can say how valued their membership was and how lucky the new congregation will be to have them.
- See if they need help packing. Bring over a casserole.
- Within the congregation, clarify the change in relationship: Are they changing from member to friend? Do they wish to continue receiving the newsletter?
- If members are leaving for another congregation or moving, wish them well and say you will miss them.
- Have a ritual of farewell for members who are moving—a good-bye party or potluck. Put a formal good-bye to them in the newsletter.
- In most congregations, the board votes people into membership and removes them from membership. It is important to formalize (through bylaws) how people are removed from membership for both legal reasons and to enhance the reality of a safe congregation.
- Enter the information into your membership database, including the reasons the person left. Use this information for archives and reference.
- If the person is still in town, and has asked you to remain a friend, invite him or her back for special events.
- Identify a time of year when your membership rolls are reviewed (often after the pledge drive or before the annual congregational meeting). How will members be notified that they are being dropped from your rolls? (See Chapter 1, "Brain: Core Documents for Your Congregation.")

MORE GOOD STUFF TO READ

Ford, James Ishmael. *This Very Moment: A Brief Introduction to Buddhism and Zen for Unitarian Universalists*. Boston: Skinner House Books, 1996. Accessible guide to the meaning of life from a Zen perspective.

Houff, Bill. *Infinity in Your Hand: A Guide for the Spiritually Curious*. Boston: Skinner House Books, 1993. Great handbook for exploring knowledge, discipline, self-discovery, social action, and other issues of spiritual significance.

Moyers, Bill. *Genesis: A Living Conversation*. New York: Doubleday, 1997. A "living conversation" that features some of the great writers and thinkers of our day discussing the moral, literary, and personal meanings of the stories of the Bible. Also available on audio cassette. (New York: Bantam Books-Audio, 1996.)

Schaller, Lyle E. *Looking in the Mirror. Self-appraisal in the Local Church*. Nashville, TN: Abingdon Press, 1984. A classic, easy-to-read book on church growth and organizational development.

Schaller, Lyle E. *44 Steps up off the Plateau*. Nashville, TN: Abingdon Press, 1993. If your congregation is stuck on a plateau, this is the book for you.

Taylor, Jeremy. *When People Fly and Water Runs Uphill: Using Dreams to Tap the Wisdom of the Unconscious*. New York: Warner Books, 1993. Shows readers how to remember and interpret dreams, how to establish a dream group, how to understand the symbolism of dreaming, and more.

_____. *Dream Work: Techniques for Discovering the Creative Power in Dreams*. Mahway, NJ: Paulist Press, 1984. Practical suggestions for improving dream recall and recording dreams. Includes individual, group, and community techniques for discovering the multiple meanings found in every dream.

Skeleton

Congregational Structures

Consider the skeleton. Consider it as armature, structure. Everything in the body hangs on the skeleton. Even though the skeleton is below the surface, it defines the shape of the body. Like the human body, the congregational body has a structure, which is its skeleton. On it hang the spirit, ministry, and good work of the congregation.

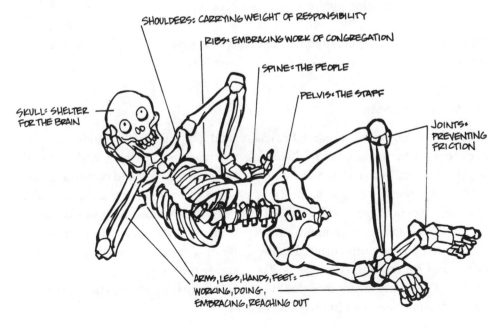

SHOULDERS: CARRYING WEIGHT OF RESPONSIBILITY

RIBS: EMBRACING WORK OF CONGREGATION

SPINE: THE PEOPLE

PELVIS: THE STAFF

SKULL: SHELTER FOR THE BRAIN

JOINTS: PREVENTING FRICTION

ARMS, LEGS, HANDS, FEET: WORKING, DOING, EMBRACING, REACHING OUT

Have you ever broken a bone? When you break a bone, how does it affect the rest of the body? When the body ages and the bones get brittle, how does that affect the body? The glory of modern science is that now bones can be replaced. Broken bones, when mended, can grow strong again.

The body requires bones to be strong to truly support it. When one bone is broken the rest of the body must compensate. As the bone mends, the rest of the body stops accommodating. Whole, healthy, and complete skeletons encourage the body to function effectively. The more the bones are used, the stronger they become. Even in extreme old age, exercise encourages stronger bones and better health. Our body's bones work together and are complementary. Imagine the structural organization of your congregation as its skeleton:

". . . the foot bone's connected to the leg bone . . ."

- enabling and supporting individual spiritual growth
- democratic, so it strengthens polity
- reflecting Unitarian Universalist values
- operating in accordance with Unitarian Universalist Principles and Purposes
- open, visible, and accessible
- encouraging justice, equity, and compassion.

How does your congregational structure do all this? Consider all the skeletal parts.

THE SPINE AS MEMBERS

A healthy spine is flexible, stretches easily, and keeps the body moving. As the backbone of the congregation, it carries out mission, covenant, and goals. It supports the collective vision of the congregation, its culture and constituencies.

A spineless congregation lacks a sense of mission, a shared vision, a covenant, operating more like a social system and less like a religious community. To develop a strong spine, a congregation regularly references its mission. It is posted prominently, printed in the order of service, and sits in front of the board and committees at meetings. The congregation visits and revisits it and renews it regularly, every three to five years. Our mission defines how we carry out our vision, now and in the years to come.

THE JOINTS: PREVENTING FRICTION BETWEEN BONES

Joints prevent friction between congregational bones. They are lubricated by good will, openness, and cooperation, by shared values, knowledge, and history, and by courtesy, affection, and kindness. They are flexible, adaptable, and adjustable. They can hinge, bend, and pivot. In a congregation with strong, healthy joints, groups and committees come together without friction. It is a pleasure to be a member. It is easy for visitors to see that the body is healthy, moves easily, gracefully, and purposefully.

THE SHOULDERS: CARRYING THE WEIGHT OF RESPONSIBILITY

Sometimes people say, "How about serving on the board? You don't have to do much besides going to meetings every now and then."

They are wrong. The board of any congregation does a lot of work and should do a lot of work. The word "trustee" has to do with trust: The members of the congregation have entrusted their board to:

- carry the vision of the congregation
- see that the mission of the congregation is developed and implemented and that its goals are carried out in a timely, effective way
- consider matters of congregational policy
- delegate responsibility for the work of the congregation
- review and evaluate the work of the congregation
- ensure that the congregation meets its financial and legal responsibilities.

Further, each board member is obligated to:

- *Attend and participate in all board meetings and congregational events.* Most bylaws provide for dismissal if a member has three unexcused absences from board meetings during one year. A board member who has been absent twice may wish to consider resigning from the board in favor of someone who has more time.
- *Accept legal responsibility* for being informed about and supporting the

actions and decisions made by the board whether present at the meetings or not. An absent board member may be able to vote by proxy, express their dissenting opinions in writing after receiving minutes, and may request that such opinions be recorded.

- *Serve actively* as a member of such committees as appointed to.
- *Be a leader in giving* and asking for financial support of the congregation from others. A board member should give a stretch pledge, that is, generously within his or her means. This modeling enhances the congregation's ability to meet fundraising goals.
- *Be a member of the congregation* who is sympathetic to the congregational mission and the Unitarian Universalist Association Principles and Purposes.

Here is a checklist for individual board members to use in monitoring their performance. (Answer *yes* or *no*.)

- I understand and accept the congregation's philosophy.
- I understand and accept the congregation's position on affirmative action and equal employment opportunity.
- I understand and accept the board's obligation to abide by the bylaws and policies of the congregation.
- I am a pledging member of the congregation.
- I am willing to be trained.
- I will take the initiative to be well informed about the current work of the board. I will come to board meetings prepared, having read materials in board mailings prior to the meetings.
- I will attend all board meetings, for I accept the responsibility to assure a quorum.
- I will attend all congregational meetings.
- I will assume leadership in giving and asking others to give to support the congregation financially.
- I will participate actively in discussion and debate.
- I will be familiar with parliamentary procedure, including the ability to frame and write motions before I make them.
- I will conduct myself courteously and with respect for my fellow

board members.

- I understand the necessity for, and will keep the confidentiality of, the board's work until it is released for general information.
- I will try to understand and question any actions that pertain to the board's legal responsibilities.
- I will abstain from any actions that might lead to a conflict of interest.
- I will work cooperatively with other lay leadership, staff, and the minister in carrying out delegated responsibilities.
- I understand the clearly defined boundaries between myself as a board member, the staff, the minister, and other congregational leaders.

Board members, like other congregational leaders who have job descriptions, set terms of office and accountability and need recognition and check-ups on performance. They can receive these through retreats and planning days.

Retreats are best when there is an outside facilitator; that way all board members (and the minister and other leaders) can participate equally in the process. Also, a true facilitator should have no investment in the agenda or outcomes. Call your District Office for facilitator suggestions.

All board members should have board manuals—see Chapter 1, "Brain: Core Documents for Your Congregation." Often, at an annual meeting or at a special conference, your district will facilitate a board training or offer leadership classes for board members. Avail yourself of these opportunities, especially if you are isolated or do not have local board training resources.

Board Membership and Composition

Although the board functions as a body, its members are elected as individuals. Members of a board are selected because of their belief in and commitment to the institution, their experience, and their knowledge of the work involved. Nominees need to be selected so that the board accurately reflects the diversity of the membership: age, gender, whether single or part of a family, theological or philosophical views, length of membership, and so on. However, board members are not chosen to represent a particular group or interest; rather, they are committed to the whole of the congregation. Some congregations ask that prospective board members agree to participate in training and/or an annual retreat before accepting the nomination.

The Nominating Committee

Usually elected by the membership of the congregation, the Nominating Committee presents a diverse slate of nominees to membership at the annual meeting of the congregation. Terms of office vary as to tenure and repeatability—see Chapter 1, "Brain: Core Documents for Your Congregation" for more ideas on the Nominating Committee.

The Nominating Committee can draw enthusiastic people and their talents into congregational life. Nominating Committee members are usually selected because they have served the congregation in a leadership role, know a lot of people, are good with people, and represent the diversity of the congregation. The most effective nominating committees do the following:

- interview board prospects personally and in a leisurely way; tell prospects that they are being considered because the committee thinks they will be good at the job;
- are candid about expectations of time and energy;
- present candidates with a packet about board work (job description, bylaws, board minutes, the budget, the long-range plan, etc.);
- answer questions and commit to calling potential nominees back to see if they will serve.

The Nominating Committee should keep a file of its best prospects, noting when someone says, "Ask me again next year."

THE RIBS: EMBRACING THE WORK OF THE CONGREGATION

The key lay leaders in a congregation hold the work of the congregation together, supporting and nurturing it. These people are committee chairs, volunteers, people who are generous with their time and talent. Here are some principles that inform the work of the leader.

Twenty Ways to Be a Better Leader

1. Clarify and be explicit about the roles of the leader and participants or the committee chair and members.
2. Be sure that all the group members understand their roles and responsibilities. Make sure everyone has pencil and paper, so they can make notes.
3. Rotate leadership when you can and when it is appropriate. Shared leadership means shared power.
4. Start and end on time. Have a timed agenda and take turns being a timekeeper.
5. Know the difference between being a leader and a facilitator and when to be each one. A facilitator must remain objective and midwife a meeting; a leader has opinions and the freedom to express them appropriately during a meeting.
6. Know the difference between different kinds of agenda items and when and how to combine them. Agenda items fall into one of these categories: decision making, problem solving, informational (reports), planning, and reacting or evaluating. Be sure each item is clearly defined and understood. Informational items should be mailed to members ahead of time, so they can be read in advance.
7. Deal with one item at a time. Bring the group back to the agenda item under consideration and ask them to table other items to new business or the next meeting.
8. If people digress, call them back to the topic. Digressions lose time and create boredom.
9. Remember that a leader's power to promote ideas and to evaluate others' ideas is profound—and too often divisive.
10. Don't set yourself up in competition with the members of the

group. You are there to lead and facilitate, to enable and empower, not to impose your will.

11. People will look to you for your leadership, opinion, and affirmation. Don't abuse this power. They may do as you prefer not because they believe in it, but because they want to please you. Try not to say what you think people will want to hear because it is easy or safe. Be a compassionate truth teller. Integrity and courage are attributes of great leaders.

12. Encourage the exploration and development of creative ideas. Ask people to explore the possibilities of ideas your group is considering. Focus on the most achievable and useful aspects first, then deal with the less useful and more difficult ones. Good ideas are built; commitment to them greatly enhances the possibility of their success.

13. Try to convert opinions or questions into actionable proposals. Opinions tend to bring forth contrary or different opinions. These are rarely actionable and too often result in conflict. Increase the probability of problem solving by saying, "I hear an opinion—do you have a suggesion?"

14. Discourage interruptions and don't accept discourtesy. Make agreements (see Chapter 9, "Liver: Dealing with Congregational Conflict") about how your committee, task force, or working group will conduct itself, and stick to those agreements. If there is discourteous behavior, intervene and refer to your agreement.

15. Do not tolerate put-downs, gossip, or personal criticism. Try to identify what is behind an attack by asking the person to convert it to a suggesion.

16. Do not let the group gang up on one or more people who are or are not members of the group.

17. Don't let yourself get "triangled." If someone complains to you about another person, insist that they speak to that person directly. If they are afraid to, say that you will go with them, but will not take sides. If they are still unwilling, ask them firmly but kindly to stop talking about other people when they are not present.

18. Use a group memory when you can: It helps focus the group on the subject.

19. See that meeting minutes are accurate, distributed promptly, and include all decisions and action items. Send a copy of the minutes to the board liaison, if you have one.
20. Finally, be open to change and willing to hear, experiment, and try new things. Be willing to stand on principle, even if your stand is unpopular. Be courageous. In *Profiles in Courage,* John F. Kennedy said that it is easy to do the popular thing; to do the unpopular thing when you believe in it takes real courage.

ARMS AND LEGS, HANDS AND FEET—WORKING, DOING, EMBRACING

Congregational work gets accomplished by enthusiastic dedicated groups of people. Keep the joints moving by allowing people to get to know each other through check-ins, warm ups, and a few minutes of social time before meetings.

There are several ways of organizing congregational work. Not every piece of work in a congregation needs to be handled by committees. In fact, equally useful, equally effective ways of work can be used.

Committees: Committees almost always are permanent structures, meeting regularly, reporting to the board, congregation, or a council.

Committees of the congregation, which are elected by the congregation and report to it, are the Nominating Committee and the Ministerial Search Committee. Although its members are usually chosen by the board and the minister, the Committee on Ministry is a congregational committee in that it carries responsibility for congregational communications and evaluation.

Committees of the Board report directly to the board, such as Finance, Investment, Personnel, Building and Grounds, Annual Pledge/Fundraising, and Long-range Planning.

Other committees, such as those falling under the areas of religious education, social concerns, membership, and Sunday services, are accountable in different ways depending on the congregation's structure. These committees include:

Religious Education
Religious Education Committee
Adult Religious Education

Youth Adult Committee
Library Committee
Archives and History

Social Concerns
Unitarian Universalist Service Committee
Social Justice or Social Action
Community Outreach
Denominational Affairs
Chalice Lighters
Special Fundraising for Social Justice
Congregational Service Project

Membership
Membership Committee
Visitors and Newcomers
Caring Committee
Lay Ministry
Newsletter
Publications
Greeters
Social Activities
Service Auction

Sunday Services
Worship Committee
Music Committee
Sanctuary Aesthetics
Ushers
Forum (or Discussion Group) Committee

In smaller congregations, all committees (except the Nominating Committee) usually report to and are accountable to the board. Of course, smaller congregations will not have so many committees.

As a congregation becomes larger, its structure becomes more complex.

In mid-sized organizations and large congregations, relationships with clergy and staff become more particular and a Congregational Program Council will be formed. This council usually meets two to four times a year and has a representative from each committee. The council reports to the board and is often chaired by the vice president of the board.

In large congregations, each area may have a sub-council, which has a chair (elected or appointed). The chairs of each area (religious education, social concerns, membership, and Sunday services) meet regularly with a board member (usually the vice president) to inform the board of their work. Committees have job descriptions, goals, annual plan of work, and achievable, measurable objectives. They have dynamic, changing membership. Their chair is usually appointed by the board and has a set term of office.

Teams, unlike committees, may pull together a group of people who meet less frequently to do a specific task. Team members bring particular skills to the task. For instance, a Publications Team might assess and evaluate congregational publications and revise them periodically. Members of the team would have skills in writing, editing, layout, and design.

Task Forces come together (usually appointed by the board) to complete a particular task during a defined period of time. When this task is accomplished, the group is disbanded. For instance, a task force may be appointed to look into the possibility of purchasing land. When they have put together a report based on the information they gather and submitted it to the board, their task is complete and the group no longer exists.

Working Groups are usually sub-groups of the board, almost always in mid-sized and larger congregations. They gather to work on specific subjects, getting information, developing options, and making recommendations to the whole board. This saves the board the time and labor of trying to do everything in the large group. It is a time efficient way to work when there are many tasks for the board to accomplish.

The board delegates work to each of the above groups, receives regular reports, and requires their accountability. The board defines what needs to be done. These small groups bring the mission into being, taking care of how the mission gets done.

Budgets. The operating budget of a congregation supports the work of its committees, task forces, and teams. Generally speaking, it is not good financial practice for committees to have their own bank accounts, for two reasons. First, the operating budget should be a realistic reflection of all the costs of a congregation, especially the work of committees. Second, the board needs to have financial oversight of any money raised or collected under the name of the congregation. Further, the operating budget of the congregation is there to support the activities of the committee rather than the committee itself. It is important for committees to give input to the budgeting process. Finance committees that operate in isolation, and without this information, can produce an atmosphere of alienation and distrust.

TWENTY WAYS TO MAKE MEETINGS WORK

1. Arrive early to turn on the heat and lights and arrange the room.
2. Greet committee members by name, telling them how valuable their contributions are, and how glad you are that they are on the committee.
3. Provide something to eat and drink.
4. Provide committee members with job descriptions, defining the task of the committee, the term of office, and the frequency of meetings.
5. Develop a covenant on your committee about the way you will relate to one another—with attention and courtesy. Agree about what you will do if there is conflict or one person becomes disruptive. Then stick to it.
6. Begin each meeting with a brief reading related to the night's work, then light the chalice.
7. Allow time (one minute per person) for a brief check-in: Invite people to say how their day was.
8. Have a printed agenda prepared and mailed out in advance with a meeting notice. If not, post the agenda on the wall.
9. Start and end meetings on time.
10. Identify the purpose of each agenda item: information, feedback, decision required, etc.
11. If you have a guest at your meeting, put them first on the agenda, so that they can leave early.

12. Have a timed agenda. Stick to it. Table or agree to extend time on items that run over their allotted time.

13. Encourage everyone to talk once before anyone can talk twice.

14. Encourage pro and con views to alternate in discussions.

15. Record proceedings on newsprint when you are brainstorming or when the whole group needs to see as well as hear.

16. Place action items where they can be seen, on newsprint or a blackboard. Include action items with the name of the person responsible and the date of completion in the minutes.

17. Rotate keeping brief, accurate minutes. Send a copy to your liaison, if you have one.

18. If conflict arises that doesn't seem to go away, ask for help from your minister, a board member, your internal conflict team, or your district.

19. Thank everyone graciously for coming. Tell them how glad you are that they are part of this group.

20. Leading groups can be challenging, exhilarating, sticky, fun, rewarding, and all of the above. Find a support person, preferably your board liaison or the minister. You might have a support group of committee chairs that meet two or three times a year with the minister to talk about your work.

TWENTY MEETING WARM UPS

1. (For groups of 12 or fewer.) Hold a pencil in your hand. Begin by saying, "My name is (use your name) and this is a pencil." Then hand the pencil to the next person, who adds their own name to yours and passes the pencil on: "My name is Mary, and Bill says that this is a pencil." The third person: "My name is Nancy, and Mary says that Bill says that this is a pencil." And so on, around the group, ending with you—and you do all the names.

2. As people enter, give them a strip of paper. Ask them to write on the strip one thing that most people don't know about them that they are proud of—but don't sign their name. Put the strips in a bowl. When the whole group has assembled, have each person

draw one out. Their task is to find the person who belongs to the strip they drew. Give them 15 minutes, then when the group is reconvened, ask them to read the strip and identify the person who wrote it.

3. Ask people to introduce themselves, placing an adjective before their name that describes them and begins with the same letter as their name (Bountiful Bill, Marvelous Mary, Dynamite Dorothy).

4. You'll need tape, strips of paper, and pens. As each person enters, ask them to write every job they have held, on a different strip of paper. Have them put their name on a larger piece of paper, and tape the jobs in chronological order as a ladder below their name.

5. Give each person a piece of butcher paper, 6' x 4'. Divide people into pairs. Have each pair trace one another's outline on their piece of paper. Ask them to write in their feet all the places they have been and love to go. Next, by their hands, what they like to do with their hands; in their heads, what they like to think about; by their stomach, what they like to eat; by their heart, what is dear to them. Post them on the wall as everyone is finished, then discuss.

6. Have people pair up and interview each other about how they came to the congregation. Then have them introduce the person they interviewed.

7. Have people pair up. Give them crayons and one sheet of paper apiece. Have them draw (with their least favored hand) a picture of the other people. Play "Getting to Know You" on a tape player.

8. Do you remember the song, "Today," sung by the New Christy Minstrels with the line, "You'll know who I am by the song that I sing…?" Have each person (in groups of 12 or fewer) bring a cassette tape with the song that says best who they are. Play each cut, one at a time. Give each person a minute or two to introduce their song, saying why it is important to them.

9. Put a map on the wall. Ask each person to place an adhesive dot on the places their grandparents came from, then, tell about it.

10. Ask the group, going around the room, to introduce themselves by giving their first, middle, and last names and then saying how they got their names. ("My name is River May Carter. My first name is a chosen name—I always loved rivers. My second name is my

grandmother's name; and I guess Carter comes from a family that built carts.") You should go first, using your own names as a model.

11. Ask each person to draw a rock or flower (from a collection you have placed) and tell what their hopes are for the meeting.

12. Have people check in by saying their name and what they had to give up or leave behind in order to be there.

13. Ask each person to think of the character in fiction, history, or mythology with whom they most closely identify. Then ask them to tell the group who they chose and why.

14. Teach hymn #402, "From You I Receive, to You I Give," in *Singing the Living Tradition.* Ask people to face each other and, looking into one another's eyes, clasp hands.

15. Ask people to bring an object that is sacred or very important to them to the meeting. Have them introduce themselves by showing the object and saying why it was important.

16. Tell people to imagine that their house is on fire and they can only take one thing out of it. Ask them to bring that thing to the next meeting and to say why they chose it.

17. Ask people to bring a baby picture of themselves. Put the pictures on the wall and ask them to guess who belongs to which picture.

18. Ask people to bring a picture of their parents. Put the pictures on the wall and ask them to guess who belongs to each set of parents.

19. Ask people to imagine they are stranded on a desert island and they can have only three books with them. Ask them to choose their three and share their list.

20. Form a circle. Have each person put their hands on the shoulders of the person in front of them and give them a gentle massage on neck and shoulders. After a minute or two, have them face the opposite direction and repeat the massage.

TWENTY TIPS FOR RECORDING ON NEWSPRINT

1. Plan how you will organize the proceedings ahead of time. Figure out how much paper you will need.

2. Put the paper on the wall ahead of time.

3. Cut or tear off pieces of masking tape ahead of time.

4. Sometimes a huge piece of 4' x 6' or 8' butcher paper is more useful and effective than a newsprint pad.

5. Use water-based marking pens—they don't smell and they won't bleed through the paper.

6. Do graphics ahead of time, titling pages and making the central points the group will cover.

7. Create the agenda and post it, or ask the group to develop the agenda while you record it.

8. Be sure everyone is seated so that they can see the newsprint.

9. Number your pages, so you can transcribe them later.

10. Print everything in capital letters.

11. Use asterisks in front of each idea.

12. Record the words large enough so that they can be read at the back of the room.

13. Use arrows, stars, or exclamation points to emphasize special points.

14. Emphasize by drawing a box around or circling a particular set of ideas.

15. Underline the most important ideas in contrasting colors.

16. Use more than one color. Four or five colors are best. When you begin, remove the caps and have the pens in your hand or nearby so you can switch easily.

17. Alternate pen colors with each thought.

18. Keep things simple. Keep them spacious. Use lots of white space.

19. Do not interject your own ideas—always check with the person who made the point.

20. Things don't have to be linear. You can record horizontally, or use a "mind map" that connects and clusters ideas like a spider web.

TWENTY GREAT PIECES OF MUSIC FOR MEETINGS AND WORKSHOPS

For beginnings:
1. Vivaldi, *The Four Seasons*
2. Stan Getz, *Jazz Samba*

3. Classical guitar music
4. Shubert, *The Trout Quintet*
5. Enya, *Watermark*
6. *Spanish Guitar Music,* John Williams (or Carlos Montoya)
7. *Gregorian Chant,* Benedictine Nuns of St. Cecilia's Abbey

For meditation or focusing:
8. George Winston, *Winter into Spring*
9. Tony Scott, *Music for Zen Meditation*
10. Khitaro, *Silk Road*
11. Georgia Kelly, *Harp & Soul*
12. John Rainer, *Songs of the Indian Flute*
13. William Ackerman, *Passage*

For endings:
14. The Gypsy Kings—any music
15. Loggins & Messina, *The River Run*
16. Louis Armstrong, *It's a Wonderful World*
17. "The Best of Times Is Now," from *Le Cage aux Folles*
18. "One!" from A *Chorus Line*
19. Kate Wolf, *Give Yourself to Love*
20. Vivaldi, *The Four Seasons*

CONGREGATIONAL STAFF: SUPPORTING, CONNECTING, AND CARRYING POSSIBILITIES

The congregational staff supports and carries the work of the congregation just as the pelvis supports and carries the body. Without a pelvis, the body collapses. In smaller congregations, devoted volunteers carry out this function. As a congregation increases in size, it becomes important to call a minister and hire staff. The larger the congregation, the stronger the staffing needs to be.

The congregational staff, the minister, the religious educator, the music director and organist, the membership director, the administrator or secretary, the bookkeeper and others who work in the office, the sextant and maintenance staff, all need support and nurturing. Any congregation that operates under principles such as those of Unitarian Universalist congregations must strive to be a fair, kind, and responsible employer.

Fair compensation, useful job descriptions, clear agreements about the terms and conditions of employment including hours of work, compensation, supervision, required staff meetings, and benefits should all be part of a congregational personnel policies book (see Chapter 1, "Brain: Core Documents for Your Congregation"). Personnel policies, orientation and training on equipment, and an appropriate working environment that has space and is aesthetically pleasing are all part of responsible employment. The Unitarian Universalist Association has published a study on fair congregational compensation practices within the denomination, *Clergy and Church Staff Compensation*. It describes the levels of compensation in reference to the size of the congregation, experience, and years of service. If a congregation is not fairly compensating its employees, it should develop a plan to move salaries and benefits to parity as soon as possible. Each district has a compensation consultant who can help you develop a plan. Call your District Office for information and referral.

Each congregation develops paid staff positions differently. If you would like help defining the position or setting salaries, see if someone in your congregation has experience in personnel. If no one is available, call your District Office for assistance.

For descriptions of ministry positions, see Chapter 8, "Heart: Creating and Nurturing Ministry." If you are about to search for a minister, call the District Office, which will put you in touch with your District Ministerial Settlement Representative. *The Settlement Handbook* describes the process.

Evaluations are important. The best evaluations are kind and helpful to the person being evaluated. Every staff person should know who to report to (the person or committee who evaluates them, usually the person or committee who hires and fires) and should meet regularly with that person or committee—usually monthly.

THE CARE AND GROWTH OF CONGREGATIONAL STRUCTURES

If yours is a growing congregation, remember what it's like to move from babyhood to childhood to adolescence and finally to adulthood. In such a way, congregational structures stretch and grow. The UUA Extension Office has put together the following Development Task Chart for Congregations. What size is your congregation now? What size is it moving toward? This chart will help you to imagine your future and plan for growth.

Membership of 10 to 50

- *Physical Space:* Meeting space appropriate for a small group; inviting and accessible. Usually a rented facility.
- *Organizational Structure:* Structure congruent with needs and involving all members. An executive committee of officers elected for one year, plus ad hoc task groups for various needs.
- *Leadership:* Lay leaders with vision and the ability to include everyone. Plan to develop ongoing leadership, not to depend on the same people.
- *Program:* Sunday morning programs weekly or biweekly. Program is expressive of Unitarian Universalist identity and planned for the total group.
- *Finance:* Clear understanding of financial needs on the part of the membership. Sharing through voluntary contributions (average $350-500 per pledging unit).

Membership of 50 to 100

- *Physical Space:* Regular meeting place, which may be rented, clearly public, well located, indicating the identity of the group. Commitment of money and energy for present maintenance and future permanent space. Consider parking needs.
- *Organizational Structure:* Keep structure simple and flexible, enabling increased complexity and continuity. Governing board consisting of officers elected for two-year terms and chairs of standing committees with one-year terms.
- *Leadership:* Active rotating core of leadership, plus several short- or long-term teams. Expenses paid for volunteer leaders. May be a part-time salaried coordinator. Use of consulting and visiting ministers.
- *Program:* Services weekly. Appeal to increasing diversity without losing your uniqueness. Find a style for Sunday mornings. Involve the total group in planning for children and youth.

- *Finance:* Budget-building related to program and shared by total group. Sunday collection; pledges on an annual basis. May have special fundraiser (average $550-700 per unit).

Membership of 100 to 200

- *Physical Space:* A "home of our own" purchased or built for the congregation. Agreement on plans, involvement of all in ownership through work, money, decision making. Room to grow as needed. Adequate off-street parking.
- *Organizational Structure:* Governing board composed of officers and trustees elected for two- or three-year rotating terms. Trustees serve as liaisons to committees. Board serves as central clearinghouse and policy-making body. Committee chairs meet quarterly or semi-annually for program coordination.
- *Leadership:* Part-time or full-time minister. Part-time religious educator. Part-time secretary or administrator. Learn to work as a lay-professional team.
- *Program:* Consistent excellence on Sunday mornings. Religious education for all ages to enable personal growth as Unitarian Universalists. Increasingly varied programs beyond Sunday service with social action on local issues. Planning broadly shared.
- *Finance:* Full involvement and open information about budget. Annual every-member canvass. Sunday collection. Fundraisers for special events only (average $600-850 per unit).

Membership of 200 to 300

- *Physical Space:* Expansion of building. Paid custodian. Continuing maintenance and upgrading. Multiple use of building. Off-street parking for expanding weekday and evening programs as well as Sundays; well lighted and maintained.
- *Organizational Structure:* Move toward board-council model. In addition to board with rotating three-year terms, a council composed of committee and interest group chairs or regular representatives meets quarterly. Chaired by board vice president.
- *Leadership:* Full-time minister, added secretarial support. Perhaps

part-time music director. Learning to share ministry as total group through leadership team. Role clarification and ongoing leadership training.

- *Program:* Continue variety and excellence. Share worship and celebration between minister and laity. Education program planning shared by professional leaders and members. Continue social action responsibility, education, and action. Attention to individual needs, consensus on overall style, conscious efforts for feedback, involvement flexibility. Number of programs and events to attract the public.
- *Finance:* Clear communication about finances. Annual well-organized, broadly based every-member canvass. Sunday collection. Fundraisers for extras. Long-term financial planning. Bequests invested rather than spent (average $650-850 per unit).

Membership of 300 to 500

- *Physical Space:* In addition to above, ways to keep building matters from taking too much time, energy, and money.
- *Organizational Structure:* Continue board-council structure. Council meets quarterly or bi-monthly, charged with all program functions, including committee appointments (which might come from a resources committee) and preliminary budget review for committees and interest groups.
- *Leadership:* Multiple staff, maintaining team leadership involving professionals, salaried staff, and lay volunteers.
- *Program:* Continue variety and excellence. Share worship and celebration between minister and laity. Education program planning shared by professional leaders and members. Continue social action responsibility, education, and action. Attention to individual needs, consensus on overall style, conscious efforts for feedback, involvement flexibility. Number of programs and events to attract the public.
- *Finance:* Active endowment building; investments handled by special committee. Continued conscious effort to inform and involve congregation with regard to finances. Current pledges adequate to support current program (average $650-850 per unit).

Membership of 500 and Over

- *Physical Space:* May need to build more space or relocate. Plan space use carefully. Long-term financial planning for maintenance to avoid crises.
- *Organizational Structures:* Move toward multiple council model, bringing together representatives of related committees and interest groups, each council chaired by a board member. Executive committee of board sets agenda decisions before each board meeting. Free the board for policy making and long-range planning.
- *Leadership:* Active and constant recruiting and training of leaders for all aspects of church life. May add another professional (associate minister or full-time minister of religious education). Clarify lay and professional leadership responsibilities.
- *Program:* In addition to above, increase efforts for publicizing programs and developing lay leadership. Possible ongoing neighborhood program groups, looking toward spinning off a new congregation.
- *Finance:* Active endowment building; investments handled by special committee. Continued conscious effort to inform and involve congregation about finances. Current pledges adequate to support current program (average $650-850 per unit).

Remember, all growing bodies need exercise. Exercise increases bone density and strength. It makes the whole structure stronger.

MORE GOOD STUFF TO READ

Bradford, Leland P. *Making Meetings Work: A Guide for Leaders and Group Members.* Duluth, MN: Pfeiffer, 1976. A primer on the functions and dynamics of meetings.

Carver, John. *Boards that Make a Difference.* San Francisco, CA: Jossey-Bass, 1990. A "new design for leadership in nonprofit and public organizations." Speaks effectively about the appropriate roles and responsibilities of boards. A much shorter cassette version is available.

DePree, Max. *Leadership Is an Art.* New York: Doubleday, 1989. One of the best books on leadership.

_____. *Leadership Jazz.* New York: A Doubleday Trade Paperback, 1993. "A dynamic and inspiring book (that) compels you to reconsider every assumption you have about . . . leadership." This jacket copy is accurate.

Friedman, Edwin H. *Reinventing Leadership.* New York: Guilford Publications, Inc., 1996. An important and effective video and accompanying study guide about an inspiring new view of leadership.

Hotchkiss, Daniel. *The Settlement Handbook.* Boston: Unitarian Universalist Association, 1995. Vital information for congregations looking for a minister. Can be obtained from the UUA Department of Ministry.

UUA Committee on Compensation, Benefits, and Pension and the Council on Church Staff Finances. *Clergy and Church Staff Compensation.* Boston: Unitarian Universalist Association, 1997. Please call the Department of Ministry at (617) 742-2100 to order free of charge. Useful guidelines for establishing fair congregational compensation practices.

von Oech, Roger. *Creative Whack Pack.* Stamford, CT: US Games Systems Publishers, 1983. A best-selling packet of book and card deck, offering "creative thinking tools" to get individuals and groups out of a rut and into more creative modes. Great fun and a great resource.

Wilson, Marlene. *How to Mobilize Church Volunteers.* Minneapolis, MN: Augsburg Publishing House, 1983. A useful and practical look at volunteerism in congregations.

CHAPTER TWELVE

Skin, Hair, Teeth, and Nails

We take care of our bodies daily—bathing, brushing our teeth, combing our hair, trimming and filing our nails. When we want a lift or to look especially attractive, we pay attention to external matters. So it is with congregations. If your building is beautiful and well cared for, if the grounds are loved and full of well-groomed trees and plants, if the interior of your building shines with the presence of all of its members, you do not need a makeover.

But buildings, like people, age slowly. The grounds may become just a bit less groomed, the paint may be peeling here and there. The interior look, with which everyone is comfortable and familiar, may appear differently to visitors. Whether we are planning a new building or revamping an old one, we need to ask: How can we learn what looks good and what doesn't? How can we learn to see ourselves as others see us?

Here are two exercises—a Facilities Audit and a Building Visualization—for congregations that already have buildings. They may be used separately or together.

FACILITIES AUDIT

Ask the board to form a Facilities Audit Task Force, composed of seven members who represent the diversity of the congregation. They will be asked to bring a report with recommendations to the board. The board may wish to set a deadline for the task force.

At the first meeting, map out a time line: When will the external research be completed, the building audit with observations be completed, the recommendations of the task force be completed?

At the second meeting, decide who will do which pieces of the research and the audit. Divide the Task Force into subgroups of twos and threes. Plan for each subgroup to visit at least one other congregation and discretely do a facilities audit of each of them.

Develop a facilities audit form to use. At the end of this section is a sample developed by the Unitarian Universalist Association.

Once the subgroups have completed their visits, hold a third meeting to compare notes. Ask: What was attractive and inviting? What needed repairs or replacement? What did you notice first? What put you off?

Now do a facilities audit of your congregation. Be honest and objective. Look at your congregation's building and grounds as if you were visiting it for the first time. Have each member of the task force do the audit independently, preferably alone. Be thorough and careful.

In the fourth meeting, compare notes from your individual audits of the building. Put a large piece of butcher paper on the wall. Note the comments that most people shared and agreed upon. Write your report.

Base your report's recommendations on what you see needs to be done. You may wish to establish priorities—what gets done next month, in the next three months, six months, a year, or two years?

Next, do a price estimate on what the recommendations you are making will cost. Consider whether the congregation will need to hold a special fundraising effort to complete the recommendations. How much can you suggest be covered out of available funds, budgeting, or fundraising efforts? Note what the congregation's members can do themselves through work parties or making things themselves. Include these findings in your report. At the fifth and sixth meetings the report should be finalized, edited, and distributed to each member of the task force for their study and approval. Then send it to the board.

Make a copy of the report for every board member. Also put one in a folder. Include drawings and/or photographs if they will illustrate your recommendations. Be sure the board receives the report at least one week before the meeting during which it will be discussed. Be present at the meeting at which it is discussed to answer questions.

Celebrate when the work is completed. Have a special dedication service, a dinner, or a garden party.

FACILITIES AUDIT SHEET

(one sheet per area listed below)

Name of Area:

How visible is access to the area?
Is this space a help or hindrance to newcomers?
How accessible is it to newcomers?
Is it clean?
Is it attractive?
Is there enough space to serve its purpose?

Recommendations:

Areas to check:

Exterior signs
Grounds
Parking
Building entry
Meeting rooms
Library
Interior signing
Worship area
Religious education areas
Fellowship/Social hall
Kitchen
Restrooms
Offices
Other

Newsprint

Markers

Masking tape

Divide people into groups of
six or eight. Each group should
have newsprint, marking pens,
and masking tape. Ask everyone
to be quiet, to relax their hands
and feet. Tell them that they
are free to make notes as the
visualization moves along.

BUILDING VISUALIZATION

This is a visualization you can involve everyone in. Congregations that are thinking of building a new structure can adapt it. Try it at a congregational gathering after the Sunday service and a potluck. It will help you understand what members of your congregation want their church to look like.

The results of the visualization can be used separately or in conjunction with the facilities audit process. If you are on a facilities audit task force, do the visualization before you write your report to the board, so you can incorporate your findings into the report.

If your congregation is just beginning to think about a new building, the visualization is a fine way for a New Building Committee to start. The information can be collected, reproduced, and given to the architect.

Facilitator: "You are driving to church on Sunday morning. Pull onto the street your community calls home. What kind of a street is it? Does it have trees? Lawns? Flowers? Drive into the parking area and park your car. What is the parking like? Is there a parking lot? Is it paved or graveled? Are there potholes? Look toward the church building itself. Can you see the church from the parking lot? Is there vegetation? Trees? Other buildings?" (*Pause.*)

"Does it look like a place you would like to bring your children? How do you find the front door? What do the front door and entry look like? Is there a welcome table and a place to meet visitors? Is it accessible and within sight of the front door? Is there a nametag rack? Bulletin boards? Art?

"Is there anything hanging on the walls? Is it permanent? Attractive? Does it change, like a gallery? Are the UUA Principles and Purposes framed and displayed? What calls you to the service? The sound of a bell or a prelude?" (*Pause.*)

"You enter the sanctuary. Is there room for you to sit or are all or almost all of the seats taken? Are there pews or chairs? Is the seating configuration the same every week? Where do the children sit and for how long? Where do you sit if you are in the choir? Where does the choir gather and warm up each Sunday morning?" (*Pause.*)

"Now visualize the minister and staff coming to work each day. Is there space for them to read, work, write, meet, counsel? Is there space for volunteers to work and meet? Is there a coffee pot? A copier? A computer? A fax machine? How many work stations? Is there adequate desk space and lighting? If there is smoking outside, what happens to the cigarette butts? Is there a place for coats and hats? Does the Director of Religious Education have an office?" (*Pause.*)

"How many meeting rooms are there? Are they shared? How large are they? Are there sufficient tables and chairs? Is there one room that everyone likes better than others? Why? Is there space to store tables and chairs? Is the seating adequate? Are the rooms clean and cared for? Can you tell who was the last group to use the space?" (*Pause.*)

"Bathrooms: Are they clean? Are there enough stalls? Are there pictures on the walls? Extra toilet paper, paper towels? Soap? Is there a changing table? A space designed for people with disabilities? Is there a dressing room? A full-length mirror? Is there a shower?" (*Pause.*)

"Is there a kitchen? What is its shape? What appliances and furnishings does it have? Is there a closet for supplies? A walk-in? What kind of counter space is there? How many sets of sinks and how many sinks in each set? Are there windows? Where do the pots, dishwasher, and utilities go?" (*Pause.*)

"Is there a separate space for youth? Is there storage space for them? Room for overnights? Do they have a sacred space for meditation and worship?" (*Pause.*)

(Other possible visualizations include foyer, grounds, bookstore and library, meditation space, fellowship / social area, classrooms, children's chapel, minister's office, storage. Include these, with the appropriate questions, if they apply to your building or the building you are planning.)

When you have completed one or both of the exercises, develop specific recommendations, including: Who will be responsible for taking on each task, by when the task should be completed, and the approximate cost involved in completing each task. Note tasks that can be done entirely by volunteers. Submit the report to the board and ask for its approval.

TWENTY SUGGESTIONS FOR A MORE WELCOMING CONGREGATIONAL OFFICE

The Reverend Dr. Lucy Hitchcock

1. Locate the office(s) in an easily accessible, uncrowded space even if you have to move it, remodel, or build it. Have more room in the office complex than the staff will ever need. If possible, have both public and private office spaces so that staff have areas protected from intrusion, but the public experiences openness and welcome.

2. Decorate the office in a way that is attractive, colorful, inviting, and comfortable, with expandable seating, excellent lighting, and windows, skylights, and more than one lockable door. Either green plants or a view of greenery outside are a plus, both for healthy working conditions and a nurturing aura.

3. Keep the office neat and clean and obtain containers for papers-in-progress. Have regularly scheduled days to organize the files and reduce the piles.

4. Have lovely artwork, in a variety of models and textures, appropriate to a religious building. A gallery with changing quality artwork of local artists or church members is a plus.

5. Have a small table and chairs for quick meetings plus a cluster of comfortable chairs.

6. Have a library or bookstore or magazine rack. Have a coffee pot going or a pot of water easily heated up with a variety of tea bags.

7. Have a conversation area near the office for people to sit, visitors to wait, and children to be entertained with a few attractive and dispensable books and toys. Occasionally put a wish list in the newsletter for office equipment, children's items, magazines, or journals of popular and religious interest.

8. Have volunteer receptionists who greet visitors and members and answer the telephone, whose primary task is to be friendly and helpful gatekeepers. Recruit people who are responsible and approachable. Train them about confidentiality.

9. Have a pile of tasks ready with clear instructions that volunteers

can follow when not on the phones or visiting: copying, folding, data entry, phone calls about upcoming events or meetings, follow-up on visitors, checking on the homebound. Some tasks with special skill requirements may be assigned to regular volunteers such as entering the attendance roster; changing the words in the church sign; entering data from the skills and interest survey; scanning other churches' newsletters for good ideas, graphics, and calendar items; getting sermon topics or upcoming activities to the newspapers; typing sermons to be available for purchase. Have special name badges for volunteers. A photo gallery of office volunteers or the volunteer on duty makes an appreciative statement.

10. Have generous office hours, such as every morning or every weekday plus Sunday.

11. Get the word out that drop-ins are welcome. Unlock the door so that access is easy during office hours. Have clear outdoor signs directing people to the office, even if you think it is obvious.

12. Have a weekly brown bag lunch when the available staff join the drop-ins for a half hour or more. Build the culture that the church is a place to meet your friends for conversation.

13. Hire an administrator who is warm and friendly and good at setting boundaries. If office staff are also church members, clear instruction and agreement on confidentiality must be established. It is preferable that office staff not be church members because of the confusion of roles. It is a myth that a non-member cannot get to know the members sufficiently or care about the church well enough to conduct their job. The supervisor, usually a minister, can have a process check regularly with the office staff to make sure that staff and member roles are kept clear and separate when necessary.

14. Hire an administrator who is good at delegating and training volunteers.

15. Put photos of the current minister(s) and all staff in the entry hall along with a map to find their offices. Place formal photos of past ministers in a different location. When there are multiple staff, place a board in a visible place with staff names to indicate who is in or out or when they will return.

16. Have clear, consistently colored, laminated signs so that visitors are welcomed, staff offices can be located, and bathrooms found without asking. Bathrooms should be clean, well supplied with paper products, including extra articles of hygiene, with something attractive on the walls. A chair, a changing table, and even a couch around the corner are helpful extras.

17. Have brochures and other easy reading material on Unitarian Universalism displayed in a portable pamphlet kiosk in the waiting area. (The kiosk can be transported to a meeting room.) Place framed UUA Principles and Purposes on the wall.

18. Have a mail center for letters or notes to be dropped off or placed in clearly labeled staff, board, or committee slots or folders. Ministers should have a way for urgent messages to be prominently displayed. Tidying the mail area is a good task for volunteers—keep a wastebasket and recycling bin handy.

19. Have a secure place for money or checks to be placed, for example, a mail slot in a well secured area.

20. Have fun in the office. Let it be a place of joy and beauty as well as accomplishment, a place of personal growth as well as spiritual meaning. Plan periodic office parties and celebrations for staff as well as volunteers.

TWENTY WAYS TO DO A MAKEOVER FOR PRACTICALLY PENNIES

1. Hold a beautify-the-building auction. Bid on jobs with time rather than money. What could you do with a little money and lots of time?

2. Have a congregational labor day. Have everyone do jobs and pay them with scrip that can purchase food and drinks. Include the youth in this day. List all the tasks, how much scrip each task will pay, and let people sign up for tasks. Have a big labor day party at the end of the day, complete with dancing.

3. Have a congregational garden party in the spring or the fall. Have everyone bring buds or plants to put in the garden. Make the front of the building and/or its gardens a glorious celebration, so that

people say "Wow! What is that beautiful place about?" Have periodic garden parties to keep the grounds fresh, cared for, and lovely.

4. Have a role-switching day—let the men clean the kitchen and the women paint a room.

5. Adopt-a-room. Have each social group in the congregation adopt a room to redo. Form a planning committee made of one person from each group to plan the overall aesthetics. Let the mini-makeovers be done by small groups, but give them all a common palette and aesthetic guidelines.

6. As a warm-up for a committee meeting, have each person share a description of the most wonderful thing about a church or synagogue they remember. Pass the word along to the Facilities Audit Task Force.

7. Have a Barter Board or a Barter Bureau where people can volunteer to work on the congregation's building in exchange for something they need, such as four hours of painting the church for four hours of babysitting.

8. Keep a skills inventory of members in your congregation's computer: Who can and is willing to do what? What skills exist in the congregation?

9. Ask the teens to organize and label (with computer-generated labels) the shelves in the kitchen or supply room.

10. Change the pictures on the walls monthly. Display the work of local artists or artists in the congregation. Include quilts and fabric art.

11. Find out who is re-carpeting their homes. Throw out the congregation's old carpet and replace it with nicer (but used) carpeting. This idea is especially good for religious education classrooms.

12. Have a flower communion one Sunday, but bring flowers to plant in the churchyard.

13. Put a sign-up list for people to bring flowers to honor or remember people. Put the honoring or remembrance in the order of service.

14. Start a memorial garden in a quiet place on the property. Plan a

landscape that is restful. A plaque can bear the names of beloved members who have died. Plant simple flowers and shrubs. Perhaps members would like to donate plants from their gardens or the gardens of loved ones who have died.

15. Make a quilt or wall hanging for the sanctuary or social hall. Organize a sewing circle that regularly sews projects for the church, such as pew cushion covers, banners, dishtowels, etc. A quilt could be made and auctioned or raffled off each year.

16. Paint the front door to the church a wonderful, new color.

17. One Sunday, display children's art outdoors on clotheslines with clothespins.

18. Move the pews or chairs and the pulpit around for a different mood or look, facing each other, or in a semicircle. Make two aisles if you only have one. Put the pulpit in the round.

19. Change the bulletin board. Put up a new set of bulletin boards in places like restrooms, hallways, entry, and so on. Ask for a dedicated group to change the materials on the boards monthly. Everything on the boards should be dated and timely. Keep it clean and readable.

20. Collect the very best black-and-white and color pictures you can find of members of the congregation at congregational events. Use photos that show faces, action, or both. Get them blown up to 2' x 3' or 3' x 5' and mounted. Hang them on the interior walls.

"Seeing the work that is to be done, who can help wanting to be the one to do it?"

—WENDELL BERRY

CHECK-UPS AND MAINTENANCE

Do you brush and floss every day? Wash your face and comb your hair? Buildings need regular attention and maintenance, too. Congregations that take ongoing care of their building and grounds have fewer cavities, broken nails, and split ends. Here are some ways to plan for and help care for your church.

THE BUILDING AND GROUNDS COMMITTEE

The Building and Grounds (B & G) Committee assesses, plans, and implements work on the building and the campus. It is usually composed of five to nine members, depending on the size of the congregation and its facility.

Use the skills inventory to find members who know about building and landscape care and recruit them. Be sure to tell them how much they and their skills are wanted and needed. If you recruit people who know their stuff—engineers, contractors, landscape gardeners, carpenters, plumbers—your work as a committee will be immeasurably easier.

The B&G Committee develops congregational maintenance plans and writes the Maintenance Manual. It contracts for, oversees, and sometimes does the work. It recommends expenditures to the board through a Maintenance Plan.

A MAJOR MAINTENANCE PLAN

Every congregation that owns a building should have a major maintenance plan developed by the Building and Grounds Committee, although a special task force could be appointed. The plan has specific implications for long-range financial planning and for the development of maintenance reserves. The plan lists:

- the elements of the building that need regular attention
- the year they were originally built or purchased
- their original cost
- their total annual cost
- their anticipated life
- their annual maintenance cost
- their annual depreciation rate
- their maintenance needs and that projected cost
- the period or interval between anticipated maintenance needs
- the year they are expected to run out, break, or need replacement
- the replacement cost
- the next time (year or month) they will need maintenance
- the next time (year or month) they will need replacement.

These items, their costs, due dates, and accountabilities should be specified on a spreadsheet for the board and the B&G Committee. If you don't have a spreadsheet template, ask a neighboring church, your District Office, a camp, or a condominium association to share one with you to use as a model.

Maintenance plans should last for 20 years and be reviewed and adjusted every five years. Examine what you want and need. Recommend that each month the board set aside money from the operating budget to be deposited in a Maintenance Reserve Fund. This way your congregation can practice good financial health while it plans for the future of its building.

The Maintenance Manual

The Maintenance Manual is a large (three inch), three-ring, looseleaf notebook with plastic three-ring pockets. A Maintenance Manual contains information that anyone needs to know about the schematics and operation of the building, including its appliances and systems. The manual and its contents are described in greater detail in Chapter 1, "Brain: Core Documents for Your Congregation."

One copy of the manual should be kept in the building at all times and one copy should be kept outside the building. Make sure the building copy is easily available. Don't let people take that copy out of the building. Other copies may be held by B&G Committee members and/or the building maintenance staff. A safety deposit box or a fireproof safe is a good place for another copy. You may also wish to include computer disks containing the original files so that you can reproduce it quickly.

Construction Planning

If your congregation plans to remodel, to build an addition or a new building, you'll be working hard. A capital campaign is almost always necessary unless you have a donor of great heart and resources. For more information about capital fundraising, see Chapter 13, "Stomach: Financial Nourishment and Stewardship."

You also can consult with other congregations that have recently undertaken building projects, with the Unitarian Universalist Association Office of Building Programs, or call your District Office for referrals.

MORE GOOD STUFF TO READ

Gallagher, Winifred. *The Power of Place.* New York: Poseidon Press, 1993. A beautifully written book on how our surroundings shape our thoughts, emotions, and actions. A must read before you call an architect.

Lee, Robert A. *First Impressions: How to Present an Inviting Church Facility.* Nashville, TN: Abingdon Press, 1993. Information on evaluating the present and future needs of members, determining whether you have an inviting environment, and making creative, cost-effective changes.

CHAPTER THIRTEEN

Stomach

Financial Nourishment and Stewardship

Imagine you've been exercising all day. Gardening. Running. Working hard. Hungrily, you sit down to the perfect meal. You are filled with appreciation—wonderful aromas engage your senses and you are grateful for the bounty before you. You are filled with anticipation—your body will be nourished. You eat, each bite delicious and filling.

Think about how the body takes food in, seeks the nourishing elements it needs, disperses them throughout the body: brain, heart, bones, senses. When fed, the body prospers.

Money is nutrition for the congregational body. Without money, the body cannot sustain itself. Like human beings, a congregation should not be starved or gorged—it's not healthy. Congregations need to think of their pledges in "bite sizes," as monthly sustenance for the church body, not an annual gorge. What sustenance do we need as a congregation every month, week, or day to stay healthy? What is each member's share of responsibility for that health?

Consider other animals' efficient stomachs. Would any of them work for us?

The lion has a lot of down time, then gorges. Unlike a snake, we can't swallow a monkey whole—it's too painful. Birds are constantly in motion, taking in, but that may require too much flying (fundraising activity) for us. Cows have a constant intake, a constant process of hay into milk and manure—and fertilizer makes things grow.

Feeling hunger is the body's natural signal that work is being done and

sustenance is needed. A church with too much money can become satiated and slothful. Lean living avoids problems like gout and the diseases of gluttony. But we don't want to starve, either. The goal is adequate nutrition for the needs of this congregational body.

BUDGETING: HOW MANY CALORIES DOES THE CONGREGATIONAL BODY NEED?

Experts suggest that the required minimum pledge is two to three percent of individual income. You might think that's a lot. Yet members of congregations of the religious right tithe—give ten percent of their income to their churches. Members of mainline Protestant groups average between six and eight percent. Unitarian Universalists average one-and-one-half percent.

A healthy percentage of giving, say three percent, is desirable, not because the church needs three percent, but because we need to give three percent so that we know our lives are focused on what we value and we can accomplish what we are called to do in church.

Present your budget openly and honestly when canvass time rolls around. Let people know what it takes to keep the body going. How you present the budget is important. Use the following Guidelines for a Canvass Budget Presentation, developed by K. Peter Henrickson in his book *Financial Management in the Church: Being Stewards of Right Relationship*.

- **Focus congregational attention on the future.** Present a budget picture that looks ahead three or four years. This will enable you to focus the congregation on hopes, rather than feelings of failing. To do this, make every effort to not compare the amount spent in the last year to the amount proposed for the next year.

- **Put the budget on a single page.** Leave lots of white space on the paper and do not reduce the type size. When you can do this, you have a "vision" budget that is comprehensible to those not familiar with it. It is unnecessary and unhealthy to lead the congregation to believe that it should adopt a budget at the detailed level used to manage the church. The congregation should not get into conversations about photocopying costs or long-distance phone usage. Instead, show "office costs" or "telecommunications." A large congregation might combine those items.

- **Do not show numbers with more than four digits.** The membership will not absorb numbers with length, at least not an entire page of them. A church budget totaling $75,000 to $150,000 should express $400 as ".4" while a budget of $200,000 or more should round to the thousands. (That $400 item should be included in another category.)

- **Be forthcoming if people ask for details.** It should be clear that the one-page vision budget is not an attempt to hide anything from the membership. When you present a budget at the congregational meeting, have another budget with detailed numbers available. This will probably be three or four pages, stapled together. (Show everything in that budget in minute detail.)

- **Do not show committee budgets as separate line items in the church budget.** It may not be possible to escape this completely, but be aware that presenting a budget comprised of easily identified organizational budgets tends to support a feudal perspective regarding the community. Having a program area that shows where the congregation is headed with "spiritual growth for children and youth" and

"Sustenance for the body nourishes the soul."
—THE PACIFIC NORTHWEST DISTRICT BRAIN TRUST

what that will cost is better than a line for the Religious Education Committee. The funds provided to the church are never the property of a particular committee, but are provided to committees to carry out programmatic tasks for the entire community.

- **In presenting a budget, do not undermine the message of the canvass.** We are committed to this community of religious freedom and spiritual growth. We freely and generously support this community and all the basic programs that make it a worthwhile institution. Every special fee levied on the membership is a message that the membership is failing in support of the congregation (religious education supply fees, adult education workshop fee, coffee, donation, etc.) When a vision budget is presented, therefore, it should not show increased reliance on the annual auction, for example. Nor should it discount the expectation of pledges by showing special gifts as saving the congregation. These are simply ways of softening the expectation of what the membership needs to do. If pledges need to increase by 15 percent, show it.

You can get financial advice, workshops on church finances, and references on reading material through your District Office. The Unitarian Universalist Association offers an excellent book on giving, *Fundraising with a Vision* by Edward B. Landreth, which discusses pledge drives in detail and assists congregations in canvass planning.

ASSESSING CONGREGATIONAL GIVING POTENTIAL

Here's an interesting and instructive exercise. Gather a task force of people who like to work with numbers. Use your directory to get a list of names of the members of your congregation. Next to each name, list the profession of the person. Find out from local statistics what is the average salary of each profession. List the appropriate salary amount next to the name of the person. Add up the sum of all of those average salaries and figure one percent of that amount. Your budget is probably near that amount—if it's lower, you have work to do. If it's more, congratulations.

Now figure three percent of the one percent amount. That is a very modest and reasonable potential canvass goal for your congregation. (Remember, it's less than half of what all other religious groups receive annually.)

When you hear the question, "What is my fair share?" or "What's the average pledge?" don't give specific dollar amounts. Suggest percentage ranges. Say, "We need two to three percent to meet our goal of $x." Don't be shy, but let them choose. Remember, people's financial circumstances differ.

Many people already give generously, sometimes a great deal more than three percent. Encourage some of these generous givers to go public. Ask them to talk on Sunday morning about why they give as much as they do. Ask them to tell why the congregation is important to them. Use these pre-canvass testimonials as three-minute commercials for one month, each Sunday before canvass Sunday.

There is a world of difference between a theology of paucity and a theology of abundance. A great accomplishment is to offer your congregation the opportunity to think about congregational life in a context of abundance. What could the congregation really do if it had the money?

Just as there are many ways to plan great meals, there are many ways to think about giving.

TWENTY PLANNING TIPS FOR RAISING MONEY

1. Plan a canvass dinner using the stomach metaphor as a theme. Invite a lively, talented, funny guest speaker to talk about stewardship and giving and relate it to sustenance.

2. Talk about giving's relationship to commitment. In all fundraising, the goal is to move people from an attitude of contributor or consumer to a giver or provider. Most people want to be generous and to contribute generously. Unitarian Universalist congregations are a part of the force of good.

3. What motivates and convinces people to change their giving attitudes? There is no one perfect phrase or way of speaking that will change people. You need to find out what is important to them and discuss with them how the congregation supports what they value or how it could support it if it had greater resources.

4. In giving, the big task is to get members to understand their relationship to the congregational body in new ways, to understand that it costs money to operate the congregation, and that each member needs to commit to their fair share. For instance, what does it cost your congregation to support members who make a small or no financial contribution? Factor in Unitarian Universalist Association dues, district dues, printing costs, the cost of religious education, building operations, salaries, programs, and so on. Often if people truly understand their responsibility, they will respond.

5. Be sure all canvass printed materials are clear, simple, spacious, and attractive. Have an expert look them over and comment.

6. Generous giving is a good habit. The experts say that people who give more will give more often and more generously the next time. So the task becomes encouraging giving the first time. And the second. And offer people the opportunity to increase their generosity rather than assuming they will not choose to.

7. Don't debate the budget on the doorstep. Make an appointment. Ask people about their hopes and fears for the congregation—this is a particularly effective process when a board member asks a prospective giver the questions, listens carefully to the answers, and takes the giver's concerns forward.

8. Consumers see giving as an exchange. They expect to get something (spiritual nourishment, socializing, community, social action) in exchange for their gifts. If this principle is out of balance, something will change, either the giving or the getting. Providers see giving as an extension of themselves: By giving, they are asserting their values in the world. The money they give allows them to live out these values through their religious community.

9. There are two attitudes: Money is a pool with limits, or money is a stream, flowing freely, always replenished. Which attitude do the givers in your congregation have?

10. Some members are kids at the table, waiting for the meal to be put in front of them. Some members are parents, in the kitchen, providing food, preparing it, bringing it to the table. Help people to discover the joys of being a "parent in the church."

11. Some members are cookbook cooks: three basic meals a day. Some members are chefs, approaching their task with joy, love, and artistry, a gourmet experience. Both can cook nutritious meals, as long as they can purchase the ingredients. Money makes purchasing good ingredients possible.

12. Some members have a wage-earner reality; for them income is fixed and limited. Do you live on a modest, fixed income? What is it like? How do you spend your discretionary money?

13. Some people are entrepreneurs and their income depends on a clear idea of what they want for their future. Without that vision, it will be hard for them to be generous. What is the vision of your congregation? Can you articulate it? Be excited about it? Describe what financial support it needs to become reality.

14. Some members are minimalists, asking: "How can we do this cheaper, at less expense?" Some members are optimists, asking, "How can we do this better? We can find the money to do it." Both are important to the congregation.

15. You can never thank people fast enough, often enough, appreciatively enough. Prompt, personal thank-you notes (within a week of the gift) written by the chair of the Annual Pledge Committee and signed by the minister are a must. Publish the names of the givers in the newsletter, but don't list amounts.

16. Involvement follows or accompanies commitment. People who give to the canvass are more likely to volunteer to work on behalf of the congregation.

17. Deal with "I give time, so I don't give money." Usually those who give the largest amounts of money also give time. Everyone can give something. People can decide for themselves what is a generous gift within their means. A modest gift is a beginning.

18. Offer waivers of annual pledges for those with limited incomes. A discreet, confidential committee with three or four members can process these waivers.

19. Deal directly with "I give elsewhere to many organizations, so I don't give as much here." Ask the person if they think that those who tithe (in the religious right, for instance) give only to their

congregation, or if they might also give to the National Rifle Association, televangelists, or the pro-life movement.

20. Be sure that you train your canvassers, or invite someone skilled in fundraising to train them, so they have confidence and familiarity with their task.

EXPERIMENTING WITH THE DIET

There are many ways to conduct pledge drives in congregations. Some congregations are trying new ways to enlist pledges for the operating budget. Here are two of the more popular ones.

CELEBRATION SUNDAY

This type of canvass moves away from the "every member" canvass to focus on a special Sunday, the date announced well in advance. A special, dynamic speaker gives the sermon that Sunday; music and readings and testimonials are planned and rehearsed. The culmination of this Sunday is to invite all members to come forward and put their pledge envelopes in a bowl at the front of the sanctuary.

There is careful preparation and materials; publicity and information are distributed well in advance. Those who attend Celebration Sunday are invited to a joyful breakfast afterwards, where the results are announced. Those who did not attend are invited to give in more conventional ways. A Celebration Sunday has a number of important qualities:

- The congregation's spirit of generosity is made manifest—all feel the strength of being a part of it.
- It saves a significant amount of canvassing time, which is especially useful in larger congregations.
- It serves a vision budget: The money is raised and then the board considers how to spend it.

"ROLL OVER" CANVASSES

"Roll Over" canvasses are used almost exclusively in larger congregations. A standing canvass committee is appointed; members of the congregation are canvassed on their "birthday"—their month of entry into the congregation. The canvass goes on continually, each month of the year. Each canvasser is assigned a modest call list per month. Some congregations use the Roll Over and Celebration Sunday in combination.

SHOULD THE MINISTER HELP?

Some ministers are uncomfortable with fundraising. Some are comfortable in certain roles, like speaking and preaching. Other ministers are very easy in fundraising roles. If the minister is comfortable and trained like everyone else, it is effective to have a minister and a board member go together to canvass the top givers in the congregation. This team can ask for "lead" or "stretch" gifts, which is especially effective during years when the canvass team is trying to raise the level of giving.

ESSENTIALS TO KEEP IN THE CONGREGATIONAL CUPBOARD

- *Collections Committee:* three to five discreet, caring people who can call on those who have missed pledges or are late.
- *Statements and Thank-yous:* quarterly or monthly pledge status statements with a note that says, "Thank you for your support of the good work of this congregation. Your contribution is important to us."
- *Good accounting practices:* regular audits, reliable bookkeeping, and timely statements. Readable, understandable, usable budgets. (See Chapter 1, "Brain: Core Documents for Your Congregation.")
- *Active new member canvass committee:* New members almost always contribute at a higher level than continuing members. It is important to offer them the opportunity to contribute when they become members. After new member training, they will expect to be canvassed.
- *Public conversations about money at other-than-canvass time:* Encourage everyone to give testimony about being a member: This is where I

"Money is like a sixth sense without which you cannot make a complete use of the other five."

—W. SOMERSET MAUGHAM

stand; this is what I give. Every Sunday have a statement before collection about giving, inviting one member to give their name and why the congregation is important to them. Ask the ushers to put the baskets in the hands of the minister.

- *Clear, simple, attractive, and interesting materials about the canvass, money, and the budget:* Your canvass materials should be readable, spacious, and cover only the most important parts of your canvass message. Just as you might not want to eat something that looks ill-prepared, your members might not read materials that are unattractive and uninteresting.

THE JUNK FOOD LECTURE

"A calorie is a calorie is a calorie . . . "

Not all calories provide nutrition, which is necessary for longevity and health. One of the worst junk foods in the canvass closet is the Cheap Factor. That's the problem of expecting, asking for, or giving too little money. Cheapness is a strain on the overall health and well-being of the congregation. Some congregations develop this spirit of paucity over decades.

The first step in getting rid of it is naming it. Begin by educating members about current levels of giving, then tell them about the potential for giving in your congregation. Don't name names, but share the results of the Assessing Congregational Giving Potential exercise that you completed earlier in this chapter.

Having too much money is like being obsessed with food. Some congregations have huge endowments but give little to the congregation and very little to other good causes. Some congregations with endowments give generously through foundations and good works. They understand that endowments and special fundraisers should not be used for operating purposes.

Talk straight. Say: "We members are all in this together. This congregation needs money to exist. If we don't do it, it won't happen."

When we focus equally on giving as necessary and important to our congregational lives, our lives are nearer to fruition. We want to be known as a generous, loving, and helpful community. We probably want to be generous, loving, and helpful people. What is required is a kind of spiritual practice that takes us out of a comfortable space because we choose to go to a better place.

When money is involved, it can be challenging, but it can also bring new vision and focus to our lives.

MORE GOOD STUFF TO READ

Landreth, Edward B. *Fundraising with a Vision: A Canvass Guide for Congregations.* Boston: Unitarian Universalist Association, 1997. The A to Z's of congregational fundraising, including creating the committee, recruiting canvassers, and planning kickoff events.

Henrickson, K. Peter. *Financial Management in the Church: Being Stewards of Right Relationship.* Oyster Bay Publishing, 1996. A lively and practical approach to stewardship and financial management.

Scheyer, Fia B. *Fiscal Therapy for the Liberal Church.* Franklin, NC: Trillium Books, 1997. Useful and entertaining information on building congregational stewardship, by a former Unitarian Universalist Association staff member.

Vargo, Richard J. *Effective Church Accounting.* San Francisco, CA: Harper and Row, 1989. A classic on planning, budgeting, cash control, accounting systems, computers, bookkeepers, and financial reports.

"We have met the enemy and he is us."

—POGO

UUA Principles and Purposes

We, the member congregations of the Unitarian Universalist Association, covenant to affirm and promote:

- The inherent worth and dignity of every person
- Justice, equity, and compassion in human relations
- Acceptance of one another and encouragement to spiritual growth in our congregations
- A free and responsible search for truth and meaning
- The right of conscience and the use of the democratic process within our congregations and in society at large
- The goal of world community with peace, liberty, and justice for all
- Respect for the interdependent web of all existence of which we are a part.

The living tradition we share draws from many sources:

- Direct experience of that transcending mystery and wonder, affirmed in all cultures, which moves us to a renewal of the spirit and an openness to the forces which create and uphold life
- Words and deeds of prophetic women and men which challenge us to confront powers and structures of evil with justice, compassion, and the transforming power of love

- Wisdom from the world's religions which inspires us in our ethical and spiritual life
- Jewish and Christian teachings which call us to respond to God's love by loving our neighbors as ourselves
- Humanist teachings which counsel us to heed the guidance of reason and the results of science, and warn us against idolatries of the mind and spirit
- Spiritual teachings of Earth-centered traditions which celebrate the sacred circle of life and instruct us to live in harmony with the rhythms of nature.

Grateful for the religious pluralism which enriches and ennobles our faith, we are inspired to deepen our understanding and expand our vision. As free congregations we enter into this covenant, promising to one another our mutual trust and support.

The Unitarian Universalist Association shall devote its resources to and exercise its corporate powers for religious, educational, and humanitarian purposes. The primary purpose of the Association is to serve the needs of its member congregations, organize new congregations, extend and strengthen Unitarian Universalist institutions, and implement its principles.